Values & Ethics in Social Work

AN INTRODUCTION

Chris Beckett
Andrew Maynard

SAGE Publications
London ● Thousand Oaks ● New Delhi

First published 2005

Reprinted 2005

SAGE Publications Ltd
1 Oliver's Yard
55 City Road
London EC1Y 1SP

SAGE Publications Inc.
2455 Teller Road
Thousand Oaks, California 91320

SAGE Publications India Pvt Ltd
B-42, Panchsheel Enclave
Post Box 4109
New Delhi 110 017

British Library Cataloguing in Publication data

A catalogue record for this book is available
from the British Library

ISBN 1 4129 0139 1
ISBN 1 4129 0140 5 (pbk)

Library of Congress Control Number: 2004099434

Typeset by C&M Digitals (P) Ltd., Chennai, India
Printed and bound in Great Britain by TJ International Ltd, Padstow, Cornwall

*Andrew would like to dedicate this book to his mum,
Carmen, with his thanks*

Contents

Introduction

'It seems that whatever we do is wrong. If we take action we are interfering do-gooders. If we don't – and something bad happens – we are held responsible!'

The fact that social workers often feel this way reflects the difficult and contested position that social work as a profession occupies in society, often trying to juggle competing and even contradictory demands. It also reflects the fact that social work is a value-based activity. There is seldom in social work an uncontroversial 'right way' of doing things. Values and ethics do not exist simply at the fringes of social work, but are at the heart of social work practice.

And because social work often deals with deeply personal and painful issues – mental illness, disability, the personal care of old people, the safety of children – the practice of social work has the potential to challenge deep-seated value positions on many subjects that most people do not often even have to think about. (Most people, for instance, never have to consider the circumstances under which they might remove a newborn baby from her mother, or ask for an adult man to be detained in a mental hospital against his will.) And social workers need to be prepared not only to operate in these very difficult ethical areas, but also to work with and alongside others who may have very different value bases from themselves.

For this reason social worker students need to explore and clarify their own values before they are faced with these challenges. A well-developed value base – and an ability to reflect on value questions – is a necessary tool for a confident and competent practitioner.

* * *

This book attempts to present an overview of the questions and dilemmas about values and ethics that are characteristic of social work practice. We do not claim to offer insights that cannot be found elsewhere, but we hope that we have presented our material in an interesting way and one that is grounded in everyday social work practice.

The structure of the book is fairly self-explanatory, but there are two points that the reader might wish to note:

Firstly: throughout the book we intersperse the text with 'exercises' in which we invite the reader to apply the ideas discussed. These exercises could be used in various ways – for example they could be extracted from the text and used for group exercises in the classroom – but if you do not want to pause in your reading to work on them, you do at least need to read through the exercises because we will refer to them in the subsequent text.

Secondly: we have included definitions, taken from various sources, for many of the key terms that are used in the text. These definitions are given in text boxes indicated by the symbol 📖.

Thanks to Paula Chandler for assistance with the diagrams.

PART I

Thinking About Values

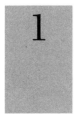

1 What Are Values?

- What do we mean by 'values'?
- Values as a guide to action
- Values and value systems
- Values and social work
- Personal values
- Societal values
- Values in tension
- Values and ethics

This chapter aims to explore what is meant by 'values' and to look at different kinds of 'values'. We will also consider the meaning of the word 'ethics' and its relationship with 'values'. Before reading any more of what we have to say about these questions, however, you might like to take stock of your own ideas.

Exercise 1.1

a) The word 'value' is used in a number of different ways. Write down as many different ways as you can think of.
b) What definition of the word 'value' can you come up with?
c) What do you think that 'values' means in the context of social work?

Comments on Exercise 1.1

We won't speculate here about what you might have come up with because really the whole of this book represents our own thoughts about these kinds of questions. Our own thoughts about values, and our selection of topics to be covered in this book, are of course themselves not 'value-free' and it may well be that you prefer your own definition of the word 'value' to ours.

What do we mean by values?

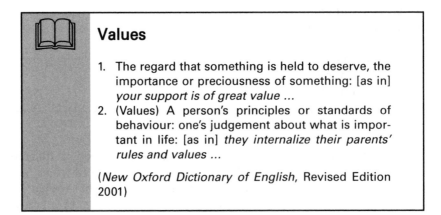

Values

1. The regard that something is held to deserve, the importance or preciousness of something: [as in] *your support is of great value ...*
2. (Values) A person's principles or standards of behaviour: one's judgement about what is important in life: [as in] *they internalize their parents' rules and values ...*

(*New Oxford Dictionary of English*, Revised Edition 2001)

The word 'value' is used in a number of ways which, at first sight, do not seem to have a huge amount in common. It is used in a financial way, as in 'gold has a higher value than lead', or in a personal way, as in 'I value your company.' Or we speak of values in a cultural sense as in 'Islamic values', 'liberal values' or 'middle-class values'. We also speak of 'value systems'.

Although 'the value of gold' and 'value systems' are very different kinds of idea there is nevertheless a common ground of meaning. It lies, we suggest, in the notion of preference or choice. When we say to someone 'I value your company', we are really saying that their company is important to us, and that we would choose their company over other things. If an expert on jewellery values your gold ring at £200, he is saying that given the choice between the ring and a sum of money, you should not choose the money unless it is £200 or more.

Similarly, when we speak about the 'value system' of a particular culture we are referring to the things that culture gives a high priority or importance to when making choices. In a liberal democracy, for instance, a high value is given to personal freedom. ('Everyone has the right to liberty,' says the European Convention on Human Rights.) In other societies personal freedom may be seen as less important than other things, such as observance of religious rules, or family loyalty, or social cohesion. We cannot say that one set of values is 'better' than another in any objective sense. We can only note that different cultures use different sets of criteria to make choices, presumably as a result of different circumstances and different traditions.

Values as a guide to action

If all the meanings of the word 'value' relate, as we have suggested, to the idea of choice, they also relate to ideas about what we *ought* to do. For example the former Central Council for Education and Training in Social Work (now supplanted by the General Social Care Council) gave the following account of what a 'value' is:

> A value determines what a person thinks he *ought* to do, which may or may not be the same as what he wants to do, or what is in his interest to, or what in fact he actually does. Values in this sense give rise to general standards and ideals by which we judge our own and others' conduct; they also give rise to specific obligations. (CCETSW, 1976: 14)

In fact it would be impossible to make choices without values. A purely factual analysis of any given situation can only ever tell us what might be the consequences of different courses of action. But simply knowing the consequences will not help us to choose unless we have some means of determining which set of consequences is preferable. And that is not a factual question but a matter of values.

To give an illustration: imagine you are driving to an important meeting – about, say, the future of a child in care – to which you feel you have an important contribution to make. You are already driving at 70 m.p.h. but, due to being held up earlier in the journey, you are in danger of arriving late. Should you increase your speed to 90 m.p.h.? If you go faster you are more likely to make your meeting on time and be able to make your contribution, but you are also more likely to have a crash and/or be caught speeding. These are the facts. Your decision as to what you ought to do will be based on what *value* you place on arriving on time as against the value you place on not endangering yourself and other drivers and/or on not getting penalised for speeding. These are things that the facts themselves cannot determine for you. 'No amount of knowledge of what is the case can ever establish for us what we ought to do about it,' as Downrie and Telfer succinctly put it (1980: 22).

In the social arena the word 'ought' often carries the implication of some sort of obligation to others, a duty to be fulfilled by either an individual or a group of individuals. Holmes (1984: 71–76) posits three specific reasons which people give for the moral motivating force implicit in the 'ought' of our actions:

> (a) it is *self*-imposed, each individual having responsibility for shaping his/her own existence,
> (b) it is *socially* imposed: a society evolves the idea of social and moral obligations to ensure its own cohesion and survival,
> (c) it is *divinely* imposed, by a deity who has determined the purpose of human existence and laid down rules to enable human beings to fulfil that purpose.

The question of *where moral obligations come from* is something that we will return to in the next chapter.

Values and value systems

We have referred to the term 'value system' but not yet defined it. How does the meaning of 'value system' relate to the meaning of 'value'? Roakeach suggested that what distinguishes a 'value system' is organisation and durability:

> A *value* is an enduring belief that a specific mode of conduct or end-state of existence is personally or socially preferable to an opposite or converse mode of conduct or end-state of existence. A *value system* is an enduring organization of beliefs concerning preferable modes of conduct or end-states of existence along a continuum of relative importance. (1973: 5)

Thus, at any given moment of time we value different things, and this may vary according to our mood or circumstances, but most of us also subscribe to a set of values which is not quite so changeable and which we may be able to define: 'I am a Muslim', 'I am a socialist', 'I am a feminist,' 'I believe everyone has the right to …', 'I believe a parent ought to …'

For most of us, beliefs of these kinds are an important cornerstone of our existence, acting as a filter which defines the things we accept or reject. Value systems inform our actions, they are part of the 'emotional mobilisation' (Day, 1989, cited in Dubois and Miley, 1996: 121) that makes us jump one way as opposed to another. They shape the way we think, the judgements we make, the perceptions we hold about people, and the companions we choose to spend our time with.

Exercise 1.2

The following are examples of different kinds of choice. Think about how you would decide what choice to make in each case, and ask yourself what set of values you would base your choice on:

1   You are redecorating your home and choosing a colour scheme for your bedroom.
2   Your daughter is exceptionally able academically. A wealthy relative offers to pay for her to attend a prestigious private school, where she will be able to have much more individual attention from teachers and a programme much more tailored to her individual needs than she would at your local comprehensive. Do you accept the offer?
3   In a supermarket you have a choice between buying two packets of tea of similar quality: one is more expensive because the company that produces it pays a good price to the growers, the other is cheaper because the company that produces it pays the absolute minimum to the growers.
4   You are married. Your partner's best friend tells you that they find you very attractive and suggests an affair. Do you tell your partner about this incident?
5   You are a social worker. You are visiting a single parent who is struggling emotionally and financially. She tells you that she is supplementing her income by dealing in crack cocaine, and asks for your assurance that you will tell no one about it. Crack cocaine is a major problem in the area where she lives. What do you say?

Comments on Exercise 1.2

If you were decorating your house, one set of values that would guide you would be your own aesthetic preferences: your own ideas about what looks good. You would also be guided by your budget (which in turn is based on your beliefs about the relative importance of spending money home décor as against spending money on other things) and also perhaps by the wishes of other people with whom you share the home. How you negotiate with others will in turn be guided by your ideas about how much you should concede to the views of others, and how much you should stand up for your own views.

In the other cases, the choice you make will be based in part on your estimation of the likely outcomes of the various choices available to you. (Do you think your daughter would enjoy being in a private school?) But it will also be based on what value system you subscribe to. (Do you believe in private education?) Often these kinds of decision are difficult because they entail balancing competing, and perhaps contradictory, values. ('I think my daughter would be happier in the private school and I believe I ought to do my best for my daughter, but I also disapprove of private schooling'.)

In the last case, however – where your client admits to dealing in drugs – the decision to be made is not simply a personal one. Your agency would have its own expectations and perhaps written guidelines about how to deal with such a situation (for example guidelines about confidentiality and its limits).

Values and social work

The final example in Exercise 1.2 illustrates that when we move from our private life to our professional life, the concept of 'values' takes on an additional dimension. Value questions don't go away when we put on our professional 'hat' – far from it – but they cease to be purely personal.

All professions have to grapple with complex issues involving values, but social work in particular, because of its socially determined nature and its focus on human interactions, constantly involves judgements in which competing values have to be weighed up. At a number of different levels, social workers are provided with frameworks within which to make these decisions:

The level of legislation and policy

Various principles are enshrined in the framework of laws, policies, government guidelines and agency rules within which social work operates. These principles are based, implicitly or explicitly, on certain values, as Exercise 1.3 illustrates.

Exercise 1.3

In English and Welsh law, the 1983 Mental Health Act, Section 3, states that an Approved Social Worker can make an application for a person to be admitted to hospital and detained there for treatment only if certain conditions are met, including that:

Exercise 1.3   (Continued)

(a)   he is suffering from mental illness, severe mental impairment, psychopathic disorder or mental impairment and his mental disorder is of a nature or degree which makes it appropriate for him to receive medical treatment in a hospital; and

(b)   in the case of psychopathic disorder or mental impairment, such treatment is likely to alleviate or prevent a deterioration of his condition; and

(c)   it is necessary for the health and safety of the patient or the protection of other persons that he should receive such treatment and it cannot be provided unless he is detained under this section.

What values are implied by this? What alternative viewpoints might there be?

Comments on Exercise 1.3

The law says that a person cannot be detained simply because they are mentally ill, but only if their own health or safety is at risk, or if they are endangering others. It therefore tries to strike a balance between protecting individual liberty and protecting the welfare of mentally ill people and the public. So there are competing values embedded here, with the law attempting to strike a balance between:

- the right to personal liberty,
- the right of the general public to protection, *and*
- the right, in some circumstances, to be protected against ourselves.

Because it is a compromise, this means that some people who are mentally ill, and are unhappy as a result, cannot be made to accept medical help, even if that help would make them feel better. Those who drafted the legislation obviously felt that this was a price worth paying in order to protect liberty. This is a value judgement. You may take the view that it should be made easier to compulsorily treat people who are not able to make a rational judgement themselves about their best interests.

On the other hand you might think the legislation makes it too easy to detain people. After all, the normal principle is that a person cannot be detained unless they can be proved to have done something wrong. It would not normally be regarded as acceptable to deprive someone of their liberty just because it was thought they were likely to do something wrong in the future. So why should it be possible to detain a person who happens to be (in the opinion of doctors) 'mentally disordered', even if they haven't as yet harmed anyone?

The position you take really depends on the relative value you place on welfare and liberty.

The principles enshrined in legislation are not necessarily in harmony with one another. They can and do conflict. Nor are they necessarily in harmony with other aspects of government decision-making. For instance, the legislation may enshrine one principle, but government policy may make that principle impossible to achieve in practice.

In addition to the framework provided by the law, individual agencies have their own laid-down policies and procedures, their mission statements and guidelines. In the case of statutory agencies these will be based on the agency's legal responsibilities and the policy guidance issued by central government. In the case of non-statutory agencies, these will be generated by the agency itself. Some values will be explicitly stated; others will be implied by what is said. The following, from the website of the National Society for the Prevention of Cruelty to Children (www.nspcc.org.uk), makes a very explicit statement on the organisation's values:

Our mission

The NSPCC's mission is to end cruelty to children. Our vision is a society in which all children are loved, valued and able to fulfil their potential. In other words, a society that will not tolerate child abuse – whether sexual, physical, emotional, or neglect.

Our values

The NSPCC's core values are based on the UN Convention on the Rights of the Child. They are:

- Children must be protected from all forms of violence and exploitation
- Everyone has a responsibility to support the care and protection of children
- We listen to children and young people, respect their views and respond to them directly
- Children should be encouraged and enabled to fulfil their potential
- We challenge inequalities for children and young people
- Every child must have someone to turn to

(www.nspcc.org.uk, as at January 2004)

The level of agency priorities

If someone said 'I really value your opinion' but then never let you get a word in without interrupting or contradicting you, you might question the accuracy of what they said. What people say and what they do are not necessarily the same. Whether looking at yourself, or at an individual, or an organisation – or indeed a whole society – it is necessary to look behind words and stated intentions to get an idea of the values that really guide actions.

If you want to understand an agency's values therefore, it is important to look at its priorities *in practice* as well as its stated intentions. Consider, for instance, an agency that stated that it was committed to working *preventatively* or *proactively*. If you looked at the way it responded to referrals and found out that referrals were only ever followed up if they were dire emergencies, you would have to conclude that in fact working preventatively was not a priority for that agency, whatever it might say, or whatever its staff might like to think.

So part of the values framework within which a social worker operates is their agency's priorities and its expectations about the ways things should be dealt with. These may or may not be reflected in the agency's public statements about its values.

The level of professional ethics and professional values

Another way in which values are, so to speak, enshrined are in guidelines on professional ethics, drawn up to try and establish certain standards of conduct. Doctors, lawyers and accountants all have their codes of professional ethics, as do social workers. (We will look at these in more detail in Chapter 4.) Underlying these formal codes typically lie certain values which are seen as being core to that profession.

These ethical guidelines, and the professional values that lie behind them, set a different kind of framework of expectations around professionals which is distinct from those created by legislation, policies and agency priorities. The job of a doctor is different in different settings – a heart surgeon and a GP have very different tasks to perform – and yet certain ethical principles, and a certain professional ethos, are supposed to be common to all doctors. The same is true of social work. And it can happen that professional values come into conflict with the values inherent in legislation, or policy, or agency guidelines.

Personal values

A professional social worker – or any other professional – cannot only be guided by her personal values, but she cannot simply disregard her own personal values either. Personal values, after all, lie behind the decision to go into social work rather than into some other occupation. Many people who go into social work are motivated by a belief that it is important to do something for those who are excluded or disadvantaged by society at large. Some are motivated by religious beliefs or political convictions. Your own personal values will also inevitably influence how you do your job and the decisions and choices that you make. For this reason it is important to be as aware as possible of what those values are and where they come from. You may like to use the following exercise to reflect on your own values before reading further.

Exercise 1.4

1 List some of the basics beliefs you have about what is 'right' and what you think is 'wrong', particularly those beliefs you feel most strongly about. What would your friends identify as things that you feel strongly about?

2 Examine these beliefs and ask yourself which ones you would regard as the most central and enduring. Which would you most readily describe as being 'part of who you are'?

3 Identify some of the influences upon your life that have helped shape those beliefs. Would you identify any of them as being part of a 'value system'? If you are Jewish, for instance, you might identify some of your beliefs as having been instilled in you by Jewish culture. Or you might subscribe to a set of beliefs which you describe as 'socialist', or 'feminist'. Even things like what newspaper you prefer to read might to some extent loosely define a value system to which you subscribe.

4 Consider how your beliefs/values might have shaped you differently if you were brought up in a different country, or at a different time in history.

5 Consider how your beliefs/values might be different if you had been brought up in a different family or a different social class.

6 To what extent do you think your gender makes a difference to the way you view the world and the values you consider to be important?

Comments on Exercise 1.4

We don't know, of course, what you may have come up with in this exercise. We can only say that the two authors of this book subscribe in many respects to very different value systems, which can be seen as in part the product of personal choice and in part the product of very different backgrounds. One of us is black, one is white. One of us has a strong commitment to a particular religion (Christianity), the other would describe himself as an atheist. One of us comes from a family that has been rooted in Britain for many generations, the other has family roots in the Caribbean. As a result of these sorts of differences, we bring different priorities and assumptions to our work. (And yet at the same time, in spite of these differences, we also find that we have a good deal in common and were able to collaborate on this book.)

Having looked at your values in general terms, we would now like to move on directly to look at the way you might apply your values to a decision of a kind that you might have to make in a social work context.

Exercise 1.5

Resources are necessarily finite and social workers are often involved, in all kinds of ways, in decisions about who gets a service and who does not.

Imagine that you work for an agency which provides some financial help for single parents under pressure who would like daycare for their children. You are part of a panel which decides on the allocation of funds. There is just enough money in the budget to provide assistance to one family, and you have four applicants. On what basis should you make your recommendation? And why?

(a) The parent and child you like the best.
(b) The parent or child who reminds you of your own personal circumstances.
(c) The parent who you think is most intimidating and likely to be 'difficult' if not given the place.
(d) The parent and child whose circumstances you find the most touching.
(e) The parent you regard as most deserving of help.
(f) The ethnic background of the parent or child.
(g) The gender of the parent.
(h) The needs of the child.
(i) The needs of the parent.
(j) The needs of the playgroup.

Comments on Exercise 1.5

You will probably agree that (a)–(d) are not an appropriate basis on which to make such a decision. But if you have ever been in a situation of this kind you will know that it can be very difficult to eliminate such factors from one's thoughts, particularly in borderline situations. As to why it is wrong to make decisions on such a basis, we suggest that it is because to do so is quite literally unprofessional: we are being paid to perform a specific role for society, not to indulge our private preferences.

What about the question of which applicant is the most 'deserving'? This seems to us to be a moral judgement about which of the applicants is the 'better' person – and does not fit with a professional role. Who are we to judge in this way? In the nineteenth century, however, welfare agencies did make a very sharp distinction between the deserving and the undeserving poor.

You almost certainly said that ethnic background is not an appropriate basis for such decision-making. This is not to say, however, that specific services should never be targeted on specific ethnic groups. African-Caribbean children in the looked-after system, for instance, may require specific help in connection with hair and skin care which is different from the help required by white children. But this is a question of different needs, not of giving preferential treatment to one group over another.

When it comes to gender, single fathers are much rarer than single mothers and sometimes, in our experience, are given preferential treatment by professional services. You may like to consider this and ask yourself whether – and if so on what basis – it might be justified. It seems to us that, as in the case of ethnicity, it can be justified only if it can be demonstrated that single fathers have different needs from single mothers. (Perhaps they are more socially isolated and have less peer-group support, for instance?)

You may well have thought that both the needs of the parent and of the child were appropriate bases for decision-making. In fact, under the 1989 Children Act, it is ultimately the need of the child not the parent that is supposed to be the determining factor, but in practice the needs of parent and child often coincide.

The needs of the playgroup itself must also be relevant, since if the playgroup's needs are not taken into account it would in the long run be all the group's users who lost out. Thus, even if she is clearly identified to be most in need, it may not be appropriate to recommend a child to the playgroup who is known to present difficult and disruptive behaviour, if this is likely to jeopardise the functioning of the group as a whole.

One point that this exercise is intended to illustrate is that there are certain kinds of value judgement we as individuals inevitably make (such as whether or not we like a person) which should have no place in our practice as professionals. The appropriate basis for the kinds of decision illustrated by the exercise should be an assessment of needs. But we should be under no illusions that by focusing on needs we have somehow avoided the problem of value judgements. Weighing up one person's needs against another is a matter of judgement and cannot be done without making decisions about what kinds of needs are more or less important than others. In most situations there are also questions of competing and perhaps conflicting needs – the needs of the parent, the child and the playgroup in the above example – which have to be weighed up one against another.

Your judgements on these matters are inevitably going to be influenced by your own beliefs and your own life experience. If you have personal experience of poverty, or of lone parenthood, or of domestic violence, for instance, you may take a different view of the cases involving such things than a person without personal experience of these things. If you have strong views that small children should as far as possible be cared for by their parents and not left with professional carers, then you may take a different position from a person who believes very strongly that lone parents should, as of right, be given the necessary support with childcare to allow them to pursue a career.

It is impossible to eliminate these personal values from professional decision-making. It is possible, though, to keep our values and assumptions under review, and be open to other arguments and other ideas. And it is possible too to recognise that certain preferences or beliefs are irrelevant to the task in hand and should be disregarded.

Societal values

Some years ago, when working as a social worker, one of us was going to visit a client, got lost, and stopped to ask the way of a boy in the street. The boy looked him up and down. 'Social worker, are you?' he asked. Social workers may not wear uniform but the boy was able to make an accurate guess all the same on the basis of dress and demeanour. However much we might like to see ourselves as doing things our own way, the fact is that most of us tend to fit into a pattern, and this is true of our values and beliefs as well as of our dress sense.

Although we are all unique, the values we hold are much less individual than we would perhaps like to think. They are shaped in large part by the society around us and by the particular subsection of society in which we find ourselves: our age group, our gender, our ethnic community, our geographical community, our occupational group, our class … and so on.

We do not notice this all the time because we tend to assume that the values we share with the others around us are just 'common sense'. It is really only when we compare the kinds of assumptions we make now with those made at other times, or that are made now in other places or in other sections of society, that we realise that many of the values that we take for granted are not inevitable, but are the result of a particular and local consensus. The following is a random selection of examples of ways in which societal values can be seen to have changed over time:

- *Sexual behaviour*. In Britain, there has been a huge shift in the last fifty years in what is regarded as acceptable sexual behaviour. Premarital sex is accepted as the norm. Homosexuality has shifted from being a criminal offence to being something which MPs and cabinet ministers openly declare. This shift has not occurred in all societies, however.
- *Corporal punishment*. Fifty years ago caning and other forms of corporal punishment were seen as normal and acceptable in schools and at home. Birching was a sentence available to the courts. Now, in several countries, even smacking with the hand is illegal, although there are still countries where flogging is a normal punishment under the law.
- *Attitudes to childhood*. Historically, and in more traditional societies today, an emphasis is placed on the duties and obligations of children towards their parents. 'Honour thy father and mother,' for instance, is one of the Ten Commandments in the Old Testament. In contemporary Britain, the obligations and duties are seen mainly as flowing in the other direction, as is evidenced by the principle enshrined in Section (1) of the 1989 Children Act that 'the child's welfare should be the paramount consideration'.
- *Freedom of expression*. Almost half a century ago, D.H. Lawrence's novel, *Lady Chatterley's Lover* was the subject of an obscenity trial. Nowadays, whether we like it or not, explicit pornography is freely available in convenience stores all over Britain and other Western countries. In contrast a significant section of Muslim public opinion throughout the world believed that Salman Rushdie's novel, *Satanic Verses* was so blasphemous as to merit the death penalty for its author.
- *Supervision of children*. Forty years ago, it was normal for quite young children to be allowed to spend long periods away from their homes without parental supervision, playing with friends. Perhaps due to increasing media coverage of incidents where children have been killed or abducted, children are far more restricted now. Parental behaviour that once would have been regarded as normal, and even healthy, would now be regarded as neglectful and irresponsible.
- *The sanctity of life*. Although the idea of human life as something sacred and precious is a very persistent value, the consensual view has certainly changed in respect of the circumstances under which the

taking of life is justified, and remains markedly different in different cultures. The death penalty, for instance, was historically used in Britain as a punishment not only for murder but even for lesser crimes, but (although it is still used in many parts of the world, including many US states) it is no longer used anywhere in the European Union. By contrast, though abortion and euthanasia are still regarded by many people as unacceptable ways of taking human lives, both are much more openly discussed than in the past and abortion is legal – and even provided by the state – in Britain.

You will be able to think of many other examples of areas in which the accepted wisdom of society at large about what is 'right' or 'appropriate' or 'normal' has radically changed in very recent times, and examples too of radical differences in attitude between contemporary societies and cultures: ideas about the roles of men and women, for instance, or attitudes to old people or people who are mentally ill.

Societal values are instilled in us by a socialisation process that begins, for most of us, with the messages we receive from our parents about what is important in life but is then built upon by many other influences: schooling, the peer group and, most importantly in modern culture, by the mass media, which constantly, both explicitly and implicitly, offer us sets of values to absorb.

But even though our personal values may be shaped in large part by the values of the society around us – or the values of the part of society to which we belong – this does not mean that there is no room for conflict. It is inevitable, not only in personal contexts but in professional ones, that we will find ourselves disagreeing with other people about value questions. And it is equally inevitable that even widely held values, with which few people would disagree, will frequently *come into conflict with one another*. In Exercise 1.3, we looked at the 1983 Mental Health Act in England and Wales, and noted that it attempts to balance important yet fundamentally contradictory principles: (a) the state should respect individual liberty; (b) the state should protect the public and vulnerable people.

It is in the nature of social work that it is prone to finding itself in difficult places where deeply held societal values collide. And because this involves making compromises in which one principle is partly sacrificed for another, this can often result in social workers seeming, in the eyes of others, to trample on one or other of those deeply held values. For instance on the one hand, because it is a strongly and widely held belief that family life is sacrosanct and private, social workers intervening in families can easily be seen as interfering and oppressive, transgressing against a deep taboo. On the other hand, since it is also a strongly and widely held belief that childhood is precious and that children should be protected from harm, the failure of social workers to intervene in families to protect children may be greeted with horror and *also* be seen as transgressive.

Because these societal values exist not only outside of us but also inside, social workers need to be prepared not only for the condemnation of others, but also for powerful feelings of guilt, even if they are clear in their own minds that they have taken the best possible course of action in the circumstances. The example in Exercise 1.6 illustrates this.

Exercise 1.6

Geraldine, aged 23, was a victim in childhood of sexual and physical abuse, emotional rejection and neglect. She is a vulnerable person who has very low self-esteem, has made several suicide attempts and is very easily led. As an adult she has a history of entering into relationships with violent, abusive men. She is a heroin user. She has just given birth to her third child, a baby boy.

Her two previous babies have been adopted. The first baby, whom she had at the age of 16, was taken into care when Geraldine disappeared for two weeks, leaving the baby in the care of a 13-year-old girl to whom she gave £5 to look after him. The second was brain-damaged as a result of shaking by Geraldine's then partner. This occurred when Geraldine had moved in with him in secret, while pretending to live at another address. This had been against a specific undertaking that she made to the professional agencies to allow no contact between him and the baby in view of his known history of violence to other children.

The new baby is likely to present particular management problems due to Geraldine's heroin use during pregnancy. (The effect of withdrawal from heroin on a newborn baby is known as Neonatal Abstinence Syndrome and can produce a range of effects including irritability, sleeping and feeding problems, prolonged screaming, fever, vomiting and diarrhoea.)

Geraldine's current boyfriend, who is not the father of the baby, is another man with a history of violence against Geraldine and others.

A decision has been reached by a pre-birth child protection conference that Geraldine's baby should be removed from her immediately at birth. Because of Geraldine's history of hiding from the authorities and running away, the conference exceptionally decided that Geraldine should not be informed of this decision in advance.

As a social worker, you and a police officer are to attend the hospital to arrange for the removal of the new baby to a foster home under a police protection order. When you arrive Geraldine is nursing the baby, looking radiantly happy. She knows you, and when she sees you she smiles and tells you that this time she knows she is going to get it right and give this little boy all the love she herself never received.

How would you react?

Comments on Exercise 1.6

However necessary it was for the baby's safety for him to be taken from his mother, there can be few people who would not feel very badly about removing a child from a mother under such circumstances. There is surely no society in which the bond between mother and baby is not seen as something precious. And in any case, it feels wrong to shatter the happiness of a young woman who has experienced so little happiness in her life.

In such situations one may be tempted to back-track on the agreed plan in some way, or to dilute the painful message that needs to be given.

Nevertheless, if a decision has been properly reached, after proper consideration of the possible consequences of all the available courses of action, then it would be wrong to allow your own feelings to deflect you from carrying out that course of action – and in fact you are not at liberty to do so, since the plan is not your individual one but one that has been agreed between all the agencies.

None of these arguments, however, is likely to change the way that you and the police officer will feel about carrying out the case conference decision.

Values in tension

Social workers are called upon to perform many complex tasks that involve difficult human interactions and in some instances involve overruling what would normally be regarded as an individual's rights (for instance: compulsory detention under mental health legislation, separation of children and parents under childcare legislation or the enforcement of court orders on young offenders under youth justice legislation). In trying to come to the right decision about how to respond in any given situation the social worker struggles not only with her own personal feelings, the limitations of her own skill and knowledge, and the constraints imposed by the real world of limited options, she also struggles with a plethora of competing values – societal values, personal values, professional values and the prevailing values of her agency (see Figure 1.1).

This struggle may be experienced as conflict *within* the individual between different and competing personal values and/or internalised societal values (as we tried to illustrate in Exercise 1.6) but the struggle may also take the form of disagreements with others. It may involve disagreement with colleagues about how to proceed. (Your strongly held view might be that 'Mrs Brown may be a little confused but we should still respect her right to take risks if she

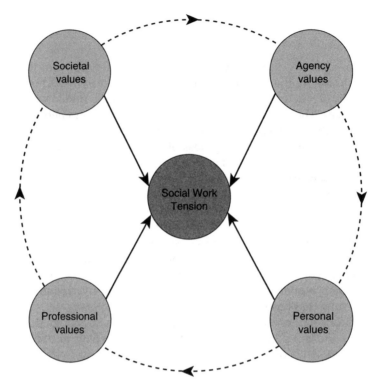

Figure 1.1   Competing Values

wants to do so.' Your colleague's strongly held view might be that 'We owe it to Mrs Brown to take steps to protect her against the consequences of her own impaired judgement.') It may entail disagreements with service users. (Your position – and your agency's position – may be that 'Beating your children is unacceptable.' A parent's position may be that 'You have no right to tell me how to bring up my children. I was always beaten and it never did me any harm at all.') It may involve struggles with managers or other agencies. There are endless arenas, internal and external, within which value conflicts are played out. Figure 1.2 attempts to illustrate these wider complexities.

Values and ethics

This book is about values and ethics but so far we have only discussed the concept of 'values' in any detail, referring to 'ethics' just in passing. So we will conclude this chapter by considering what ethics are and how they relate to values.

'Ethics' has a narrower meaning than 'values' in that 'values' can be used in senses other than the purely moral one ('I value your friendship', 'the value of gold' and so on), but 'ethics' is really only used in relation to moral

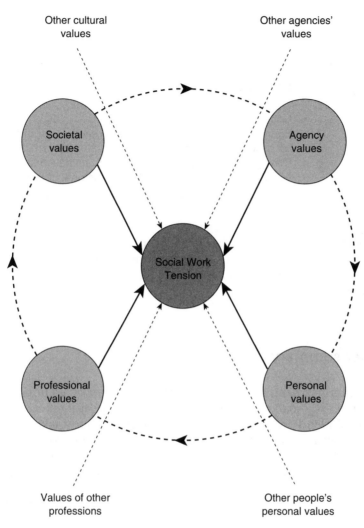

Other cultural
values

Other agencies'
values

Societal
values

Agency
values

Social Work
Tension

Professional
values

Personal
values

Values of other
professions

Other people's
personal values

Figure 1.2   Competing Values: The Wider Picture

values. Dubois and Miley (1996: 122) suggest that ethics is 'concerned with what people consider "right"' while 'values are concerned with what people consider good'. 'Ethics' is also a word that tends to be used in particular in relation to formally constructed codes of conduct (which will be discussed later in this book, in Chapter 4). Dubois and Miley suggest an additional distinction between microethics and macroethics. They use microethics to refer to a set of principles and standards that direct individual practice and macroethics to describe a set of principles that deals with 'organisational arrangements and values as well as ethical principles that underlie and guide social policies' (Conrad, 1988, cited by Dubois and Miley, 1996: 122).

The following is a definition of the word 'ethics' as it is used in this book:

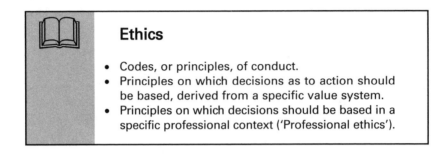

Ethics

- Codes, or principles, of conduct.
- Principles on which decisions as to action should be based, derived from a specific value system.
- Principles on which decisions should be based in a specific professional context ('Professional ethics').

There is also a more specialist use of the word 'ethics'. It is the name given to the branch of philosophy – also called 'moral philosophy' – that considers the nature of morality. This is a topic to which we will be returning in the next chapter.

Chapter summary

This chapter has been an exploration of the concept of 'values'. We have considered the meaning of the word, arguing that 'values' are an indispensable (indeed unavoidable) component of decision-making in a personal or professional context. We have looked at different kinds of values, including the values that are expressed by laws, policies and agency practice and custom, as well as societal and personal values. We have considered the tensions and contradictions that can arise between competing values, and we have related the idea of values to that of ethics.

The specific topic headings covered have been:

- What do we mean by 'values'?
- Values as a guide to action
- Values and value systems
- Values and social work
- Personal values
- Societal values
- Values in tension
- Values and ethics

2   Moral Philosophy

- Values and ethics as philosophical problems
- The problem of relativism
- Deontological theories
- Consequentialist theories
- Virtue ethics
- Values and politics

We'd like to begin this chapter by asking you consider a debate that might take place in a social work team about the right thing to do in a given set of circumstances.

Exercise 2.1

The following is an imaginary discussion taking place in a social work team meeting. You will find that the participants take different views on the question under consideration: whether or not to close a 'call-in surgery' which the team operates to provide an easy access point for members of the public. Some are in favour of closing it, some are against. What we would like you to consider is the *kinds* of argument that are presented by each of the four participants. How do each of these people seem to come to conclusions about whether a particular course of action is right or wrong?

The Greytown call-in surgery

The Greytown children and families social work team has been operating a weekly 'call-in surgery' in a school in its patch. In the

(Continued)

monthly team meeting, Richard, the team leader puts forward a proposal to close down the call-in surgery in order to free up a day per week of social work time to deal with a backlog of child protection work. He argues that the team is seriously overstretched and that, in the absence of additional resources, it will have to rein in its preventative activities in order to concentrate on ensuring that the immediate safety needs of children at risk are met.

'I appreciate that the call-in surgery is a popular resource for families in the area, but a child could be badly hurt as a result of our current backlog of child protection work. At the end of the day protecting children has got to be our first priority.'

Janice strongly disagrees. She says that, if the team is to continue to call itself a social work team, it cannot just let itself be turned into 'a sort of specialist police service'.

'Greytown is a desperately deprived area,' she says. 'People are really up against it. And we as social workers have a duty to offer support and advocacy, and to maintain some sort of links with the community, not just let ourselves be turned into yet another outside force for people to be scared of.'

David agrees with Janice that the call-in surgery should be kept.

'I really think,' he says, 'that in the long run we may protect more children by offering support and advocacy to parents than we do by going in like firefighters when the situation has already gone too far.'

Richard says this may or may not be so, but if a child on his allocation waiting list was seriously injured, he couldn't forgive himself if he knew that the case could have been followed up earlier if he'd acted now.

David repeats his view that the call-in surgery itself prevents child abuse, but Lucy thinks that he's wrong.

'Given the size of the patch and the relatively small proportion of the population who use the call-in surgery,' she says, 'I have to say I think that the impact of the call-in service on child abuse is probably pretty small. Don't get me wrong, it would be great to have a preventative approach to child abuse, but we just aren't adequately resourced for it. I know that the call-in is appreciated by many people but it seems to me that we should focus our limited resources on those in most need in order to make as much difference as possible. That means, like Richard says, concentrating on dealing with identified child protection cases.'

Comments on Exercise 2.1

Two people argue in favour of closing the call-in surgery – Richard and Lucy – and two people argue against – David and Janice.

But, although Richard and Lucy both argue in favour of closing the 'surgery', they don't use the same type of argument. Richard argues in terms of duties: he sees his duty to protect children who may be being abused as something which overrides other considerations. Lucy does not take such an absolute stance but argues that resources are limited and the most effective way of deploying those resources – in terms of maximising the benefit to service users – is by investing those resources in child protection casework.

Similarly, while both Janice and David argue against closure they also do not use the same argument as one another. Even though she disagrees with Richard, Janice's argument is, in a way, quite similar to his because she too argues in terms of duties. She feels that social workers have a duty to provide support to the oppressed and marginalised, and that this duty cannot be set aside. For her, as for Richard, some duties are, so to speak, set in stone. It's just that she disagrees with Richard about the nature of those duties. David, however, uses an argument which is more like Lucy's, even though he comes to the opposite conclusion. Like Lucy, he sees the decision in terms of a pragmatic calculation as to which course of action will bring the greater benefit. He just disagrees with Lucy about the relative benefits that each of the two alternative courses of action will bring.

In terms of their positions on closing the call-in surgery, then, Richard and Lucy take one side, Janice and David take another. But in terms of the principles which they apply in coming to a view, we could pair Richard and Janice, on the one hand, and Lucy and David on the other. They might not know it, but underlying the argument about the call-in centre is a philosophical argument dating back to the eighteenth century. Richard and Janice's way of seeing things has something in common with the 'deontology' of the German philosopher Immanuel Kant. Lucy and David's approach has more in common with the 'utilitarianism' espoused by philosophers such as Jeremy Bentham and John Stuart Mill.

There are a number of different ways in which we can consider the sources or origins of moral values. For example, we can look at the values of an individual in terms of their personal history – a person who had a very unhappy experience in a boarding school, for instance, might have particularly strong views that it is wrong to send children to such schools – or in terms of their upbringing and cultural background. We may attribute some of a person's values to their Jewish upbringing, or to their working-class origins, or to the fact that they grew up in the country as opposed to the town.

This chapter will look at questions that have been raised by philosophers since ancient times, about the nature of morality itself and its basis in reality. This is the branch of philosophy known as 'Moral philosophy' or just as 'Ethics'.

Values and ethics as philosophical problems

It is wrong to kill people, to tell lies, to break promises, to abuse children.... These are hardly controversial statements. But *why* are these things wrong and what do we mean by 'wrong'? It may seem to us that the 'wrongness' of these things is self-evident but this is *not* necessarily so. A hundred years ago, sex before marriage would have been regarded by many as self-evidently 'wrong'. Nowadays, even though some people do still regard it as wrong, it is widely accepted as normal behaviour with no stigma attached to it at all: few people would be embarrassed or ashamed to admit that they had sex before they were married. Less than two centuries ago, slavery and slave-trading were legal and respectable activities in the British Empire and in the USA. There are still elderly people alive today who, in their childhood, could have met with people born into slavery. Nowadays, it seems bizarre that anyone could ever have regarded it as acceptable to buy and sell human beings as if they were farm animals. Indeed in some countries, such as Germany, even farm animals themselves have legal rights under the constitution!) Rightness and wrongness are not quite so self-evident as they appear at first sight.

Consider the statement 'It is wrong to kill people'. In every society, now and in the past, it has been generally accepted that it is wrong to kill people, even though most, if not all, societies have attached various caveats and exceptions. In the present day some of these exceptions include killing in war, the death penalty, euthanasia and abortion. In the past they have included such circumstances as gladiatorial contests (in the Roman Empire), sacrifices to the gods (for example in the Aztec civilisation of Mexico) and infanticide (the killing of newborn babies, for example when they had visible disabilities, which was legal and acceptable in a number of cultures in the past).

Some cultures and individuals apply the idea that it is wrong to kill not only human beings but also other species. Strict adherents of the Jain religion, for example, are not just vegetarian but even try to avoid accidentally stepping on insects. But this is exceptional and we would guess that there is a majority view across the world that it is wrong to kill people, but that the same rules do not apply to animals. Indeed, many people think it is acceptable to kill animals not only for food but for the advancement of science, for fashion or even for entertainment (bullfighting, fox-hunting, angling).

Readers of this book will have different views as to the limits and permissible exceptions to the general principle that it is wrong to kill. Some will be vegetarians or vegans, others will enjoy fishing or shooting as sports. Some will be pacifists, others will regard killing as legitimate in pursuit of just war aims, or as part of a liberation struggle against an oppressive regime. There will be different views on abortion (up to what stage of pregnancy and in what circumstances?), on euthanasia and the death penalty and on sacrificing animals to research. (Is it acceptable to kill animals for cancer research? How about for testing cosmetics? Or in academic research on brain development? Or to test surgical procedures? Or to learn the effects of new weapons systems? Where do you draw the line and why?)

These differences of view are interesting and important – and present real problems for moral philosophers. Nevertheless it is probably safe to make the assumption that any reader of this book will agree that, at least under most circumstances, *killing people is wrong*.

The question is – why?

Exercise 2.2

Exactly why do you regard killing people as wrong?

What does 'wrong' mean in this context?

In answering these questions, try to challenge your own assumptions and terms. For example, if you were to answer 'Killing people is wrong because no one has the right to end another person's life', then you would need to ask what you mean by 'rights' and where they come from.

Comments on Exercise 2.2

We think you will agree that the question is harder than it appears. The kinds of arguments you use in support of the view that killing people is wrong may fall into one or more of three broad categories:

1   Killing is wrong because a human life has an intrinsic value.
2   A society could not function in which it was acceptable for people to kill one another – and we would all lose out as a result.
3   Killing is wrong because God has told us so.

Each of these answers implies a somewhat different meaning of the word 'wrong'. In the first case 'wrong' means 'harming something of intrinsic value'. In the second case, it means 'harmful to the general good'. In the third case it means 'disobedient to God'.

Of the three kinds of argument discussed above, the last one, rooted in religious belief, has provided a basis for moral teaching for millennia. It is probably still the basis of the ethical systems of most people on the planet and, in our experience, a considerable number of people who come into social work (including one of the two authors of this book) were motivated to do so partly by their religious faith. Regardless of whether or not they have religious convictions, social workers will certainly encounter people of many different faiths among the users of their services for whom religious belief lies at the core of their value system. For these reasons we have made 'values and religion' the subject of a whole chapter of its own, following this one.

The other two viewpoints suggested above on what constitutes 'wrong' are not based on religion, though, and therefore do not rely on rules provided to us, from outside as it were, by a deity. They are based instead on different philosophical conceptions of the nature of morality. Interestingly both of these viewpoints were propounded by philosophers in the eighteenth century when the role of the established church as arbiter on moral matters began to come into question.

The idea that killing people is wrong because human life has intrinsic value is based on the idea that there are moral absolutes in the world. There are things which are quite simply wrong, morally, just as there are things which are wrong logically or arithmetically. This approach is associated in particular with the eighteenth-century German philosopher Immanuel Kant, whom we mentioned in the introduction to this chapter, and is called *deontological*, which comes from the Greek word for 'duty'.

The other argument – killing people is wrong because society could not otherwise function and we would all be the losers – is an example of a *utilitarian* position, commonly associated with the eighteenth-century British philosopher Jeremy Bentham and the nineteenth-century philosopher John Stuart Mill. The utilitarian view is that whether or not an action is right or wrong is to be measured by the overall consequences of that action for everyone. Utilitarianism is therefore categorised as a *consequentialist* position.

The following example may help to make clear the distinction.

Exercise 2.3

Few readers of this book will want to dispute that one of the most repugnant forms of human behaviour is deliberate torture.

Exercise 2.3   (Continued)

But suppose that a plot is discovered to explode a nuclear bomb in a large city. One of the conspirators has been arrested. He confirms the existence of the bomb, but refuses to divulge which city has been targeted, though he says he knows precisely where the bomb is. The bomb is thought to be powerful enough to threaten many thousands of lives. Would torture be justified to obtain the information required to save all those lives?

Comments on Exercise 2.3

Two contrasting viewpoints here are that:

1   Torture is intrinsically evil and cannot be justified under any circumstances, even these ones (a 'deontological' argument).
2   Torture may generally be a bad thing, but under these circumstances it is justified because the suffering it will cause is outweighed by the suffering it will prevent (a 'consequentialist' argument).
3   It may occur to you, though, that a more subtle consequentialist argument might consider the long-term consequences of permitting torture under these circumstances and end up coming to the opposite conclusion. It might go something like this: In this particular case, torturing the captured conspirator might prevent more suffering than it caused, but in the long run it would cause more suffering, because it would allow the principle to be established that torture could be used in some circumstances – and this would mean that torture would end up being used in more and more cases, to the long-term detriment of everyone. James Rachels calls this sort of reasoning 'The Slippery Slope Argument' (Rachels, 1999: 14).

We will look more closely below at deontological and consequentialist approaches, but first we should mention the thorny problem of relativism, which often bedevils decision-making in social work.

The problem of relativism

The Greek philosopher Plato believed that moral values simply *exist*, like mathematical truths. One difficulty with this idea is that, as we have already discussed, moral values change over time and vary between different cultures. On the one hand, a person from Saudi Arabia might be shocked by the free consumption of alcohol in this country. Most English people, on the other hand, would deplore the Saudi use of the death penalty for offences such as adultery. Is it possible to reconcile the idea of moral values as deep and enduring things to a world in which there is no agreement about what is right and wrong? And if not, where does it leave us? Isn't moral relativism a slippery slope leading to a world with no morality at all, where everyone can claim to be doing 'right' according to his or her personal definition of the term, and no one will be able to question it?

This is not just a philosophical question but a practical one for a society in which many different cultures, faiths and belief systems coexist. It also presents real difficulties for social workers, who have to struggle with questions such as:

- Who am I to decide what constitutes 'good enough parenting'?
- Do we have any right to intervene to prevent practices which another culture regards as normal?
- Are we imposing middle-class values on working-class service users?
- Can social workers in the West impose Western liberal values – for example about relationships between men and women or adults and children – on people from other cultures who have strong, and very different beliefs?

James Rachels (1999: 27–9) argues that there may in fact be less disagreement about values than there seems between different cultures and that different cultural practices do not necessarily reflect different underlying values but adaptation to different circumstances. There are, he suggests, a number of basic underlying values that are shared by all societies, such as that it is wrong to lie, that it is important to care for little children, and that murder is wrong (albeit with the various caveats that we discussed earlier). This may help us to allay any anxieties we have about moral relativism being a step in the direction of no morality at all – and even perhaps makes it possible to salvage Plato's idea of moral values having an existence of their own, like mathematical facts. But it does not solve the social work dilemmas we have just mentioned.

What may help is to be as clear as possible about how values work and where they come from. The box below on 'good enough parenting' shows how we may clarify ideas about value by 'unpacking' them.

Good enough parenting

The concept of good enough parenting is a difficult one to apply. It may become marginally easier when we recall that the 1989 Children Act does not actually use the term 'good enough parenting'. The test that the Children Act uses for questions such as whether a child should be taken from a parent's care is whether or not the child is suffering or is likely to suffer 'significant harm', attributable to the care given, or likely to be given, by the parent or carer (see 1989 Children Act, Section 31(2)). Although 'harm' is itself a hard thing to measure, it is perhaps a little easier than measuring whether parenting is 'good enough'.

In a sense the Children Act adopts a 'consequentialist' view of adequate parenting, in that parenting is to be assessed not on the basis of abstract principles about what constitutes a good parent, but on the basis of the likely consequences for the child of the care actually given.

Deontological theories

Deontological theories are based on the idea that there are certain things that we should or should not do, irrespective of the consequences. This was illustrated by Exercise 2.3. From a deontological viewpoint, if torture is wrong then it is wrong, and cannot be justified by the fact that, in this particular instance, it could prevent more suffering than it causes.

 ## Deontology

Coming from the Greek work *deon*, which means duty, deontology means 'the science of duty'. Ethical theories based on the idea of pre-existing duties and obligations, are therefore described as 'deontological'.

Deontological theories are also sometimes called nonconsequentialist, because they do not measure the rightness or wrongness of an action by its consequences.

'Virtue Ethics', which we will discuss later, could also be described as a nonconsequentialist approach.

There are a number of different deontological approaches. One approach with which we are very familiar in the modern world is based on the concept of human *rights* (which always carry the concomitant duty to respect the rights of others). The seventeenth-century British philosopher John Locke, for instance, suggested that human beings had a right to life, health, liberty and possessions, an idea which was taken up in the famous text of the American Declaration of Independence, written by Thomas Jefferson:

> We hold these Truths to be self-evident, that all Men are created equal, that they are endowed by their Creator with certain unalienable Rights, that among these are Life, Liberty and the Pursuit of Happiness ...

The idea of inalienable human rights (with the concomitant duties on the rest of society) is in fact a classically deontological idea, and one which continues to be very influential. The European Convention on Human Rights, enshrined in law in the UK in the 1998 Human Rights Act, could be argued to be in a direct line of descent from the American Declaration, and therefore from the ideas of Locke. It is a piece of legislation which will have many practical implications for social work in Europe.

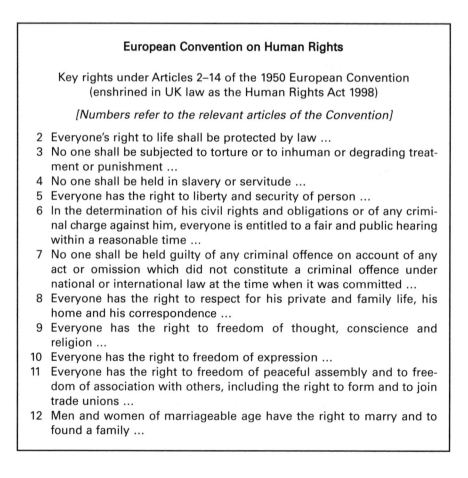

European Convention on Human Rights

Key rights under Articles 2–14 of the 1950 European Convention (enshrined in UK law as the Human Rights Act 1998)

[Numbers refer to the relevant articles of the Convention]

2 Everyone's right to life shall be protected by law ...
3 No one shall be subjected to torture or to inhuman or degrading treatment or punishment ...
4 No one shall be held in slavery or servitude ...
5 Everyone has the right to liberty and security of person ...
6 In the determination of his civil rights and obligations or of any criminal charge against him, everyone is entitled to a fair and public hearing within a reasonable time ...
7 No one shall be held guilty of any criminal offence on account of any act or omission which did not constitute a criminal offence under national or international law at the time when it was committed ...
8 Everyone has the right to respect for his private and family life, his home and his correspondence ...
9 Everyone has the right to freedom of thought, conscience and religion ...
10 Everyone has the right to freedom of expression ...
11 Everyone has the right to freedom of peaceful assembly and to freedom of association with others, including the right to form and to join trade unions ...
12 Men and women of marriageable age have the right to marry and to found a family ...

(Continued)

13 Everyone whose rights and freedoms as set forth in this Convention are violated shall have an effective remedy before a national authority ...

14 The enjoyment of the rights and freedoms set forth in this Convention shall be secured without discrimination on any ground such as sex, race, colour, language, religion, political or other opinion, national or social origin, association with a national minority, property, birth or other status.

Rights are important in social work thinking. However, when we consider our own actions as professional social workers, it is necessary to think in terms of duties. Attempts to encapsulate the professional ethics of social work (to be discussed in more detail in Chapter 4) typically take the form of core duties or responsibilities. These usually draw heavily on the deontological approach of Immanuel Kant (1724–1804). Kant believed that moral duties could be arrived at by a process of reasoning. He argued that there was a 'categorical imperative' which formed the basis of all other duties, and that this imperative was simply self-evident, rather like $1 + 1 = 2$. Rather confusingly he produced four different versions of this categorical imperative. Two of these are the following:

- Act only on that maxim whereby you can at the same time will that it become a universal law. [*Thus, in our torture example: if you believe that torture is unacceptable, then you cannot make an exception in a particular case.*]
- So act as to treat humanity, whether in your own person or in that of any other, never solely as a means but always also as an end. [*In the torture example: it is not acceptable to set aside the humanity of the arrested conspirator and use him purely as a means of obtaining information, however much that information might benefit others.*] (from Norman, 1998: 76)

The second of these versions has been particularly influential in social work ethics, since it is the basis of the idea of 'respect for persons'. 'Every human being has intrinsic value,' says the BASW *Code of Ethics* (2002: 2), which is really a restatement of the idea that human beings are 'ends' and never just 'means'. People's value results simply from their *being* people and is not based on their usefulness.

Why should human beings be regarded as 'ends' and not 'means'? Kant thought that humans should be regarded in this way because they are *rational beings*. He considered that, in principle, any rational being (including, say, an intelligent Martian) should be considered in the same way. Animals, not being rational (at least in Kant's view), 'are there merely as a means to an end. That end is man' (Kant, 1979 [1779]: 239).

✻Kant was critical of the purely utilitarian approach, because it would allow us to sacrifice one individual for the sake of others, if it could be shown that the benefits to the others would exceed the harm done to the one individual. This one individual would then be being treated entirely as a means and not an end, which is precisely the scenario that would have resulted if the arrested conspirator in Exercise 2.3 had been tortured to obtain information. The conspirators themselves would also have been guilty of using people as means rather than ends, since they were prepared to let off a bomb and sacrifice lives in order to further their cause.

(We should note, though, that real life conspirators of this kind in the modern world do not on the whole use utilitarian arguments to justify their actions, but arguments derived from religion. Examples would be the 9/11 terrorists or those radical anti-abortionists in the US who feel justified in murdering staff at abortion clinics. Others use a sort of deontological argument that duty to one's country or one's cause is sacred and must be given priority over other considerations.)

If you think about it, it would be difficult to construct a system of values if we did not, in some degree, regard people as ends as opposed to means. After all, if people could be regarded simply as 'means' then what would *be* the end? What other end is there? But there are difficulties nevertheless with the deontological approach.

Exercise 2.4

Look back at one of the ethical dilemmas discussed in previous exercises in this book – or consider an ethical problem you have encountered in your own experience.

The Kantian approach, and the whole deontological approach, is that such problems are not solved simply by a calculation as to which option will bring about the least detrimental consequences, but with reference to duties and/or rights.

What difficulties can you see in practice with Kant's approach and with the deontological conception of duties or rights?

Comments on Exercise 2.4

You will have thought of others, but the following are some of the difficulties that occur to us:

1   A deontological approach does not prevent us from having to weigh up the benefits and the harm that will arise from any course of action. Even assuming that everyone agrees on what their duties and rights are, the fact is that in the real world we constantly discover that our duty to one individual conflicts with our duty to another, or we have two different conflicting duties in relation to the same individual (where a person's right to freedom conflicts with their right to protection, to give an example commonly encountered in social work). It can also happen that it is simply not physically possible to do all the things that one would like to do or feels one ought to do. In these situations, it is difficult to see how to proceed other than by looking at the costs and benefits of the various options. Such dilemmas are everyday occurrences in social work practice.

2   The idea of human rationality as the cornerstone of 'respect for persons' also creates some difficulties since not all human beings can really be described as capable of rational thought. If someone you care about was to lose the capacity for rational thought – perhaps as a result of dementia or brain damage – would you be happy for that person to stop being treated as having intrinsic worth? The implications for social work would be pretty alarming if we decided that people with dementia, brain damage or severe learning difficulties were not entitled to respect as persons. But why should not the capacity for suffering, or the capacity to form attachments, merit respect, as well as the capacity for rational thought?

Those who are interested in the well-being of animals might similarly argue that, even assuming that animals are not capable of rational thought (which is probably not true in any case), why should this mean that their suffering is of no account?

In spite of these reservations, the concept of 'respect for persons' and the insistence that people should not merely be used as means to an end are powerful and important ideas. They are particularly relevant to social work because of social work's particular focus on marginalised or oppressed groups within society. Mentally ill people, people with learning disabilities, the frail elderly: these are precisely the groups whose humanity society at large tends to forget or ignore. Even after the closing down of most large-scale institutions, there remains a tendency to treat people with dementia, or learning disabilities, or mental illness, not as 'ends' in their own right but as objects to be 'warehoused' as tidily as possible, out of the sight and mind of the rest of the population.

The marginalisation of certain groups is often the result of policies which attach less importance to the needs of those groups than to the interests and concerns of others. When this occurs it is surely a case of people being used as means rather than as ends. When economists argue, for instance, that it is necessary to maintain a certain level of unemployment in society in order to keep inflation down, then they are suggesting that some people should be denied the opportunity to earn their own living in order to help the rest of us to prosper. Many of the people with whom social workers deal, one could argue, have been excluded from the economy in precisely this kind of way.

Horne argues that part of social work's role is to represent members of these groups, to themselves and to the rest of society, as 'subjects' rather than 'objects':

> The social worker, on the one hand faced with, for example, an 'objectified' vandal, and on the other with a legal discourse, attempts to present the underlying humanity of the vandal. (1999: 82–3)

The social worker, on this model, should be trying to make her clients visible as human beings. She should be trying to help them to obtain the respect that is due to them as persons rather than simply being seen as 'problems'. In practice, though, it is all too easy for beleaguered social workers themselves to end up seeing their clients as problems not people.

Consequentialist theories

'Consequentialism' is a collective term for group of moral theories which are based on the idea that what determines the rightness or otherwise of an action is whether the consequences of that action are favourable or unfavourable. So all consequentialist approaches require that we tally up the good and bad consequences of actions and see whether the good conse-quences outweigh the bad.

One might ask: 'The consequences for whom?' And in fact there are several kinds of consequentialist theory based on different answers to this question. *Ethical egoism* is based on the idea that an action is morally right if the overall consequences of it are favourable for the person carrying out the action (you can see that this will result in a rather eccentric definition of morality unless you believe that selfish actions are ultimately harmful to the person carrying them out). *Ethical altruism*, on the other hand considers the consequences for everyone *except* the person carrying out the action. *Utilitarianism*, the third kind of consequentialist theory, considers the conse-quences of the action for *everyone*. We will confine the remainder of this discussion to utilitarianism.

Consequentialism *and* Utilitarianism

Consequentialism: The view that the morality of an action is determined by whether or not its consequences are favourable.

Utilitarianism: A consequentialist theory based on the idea that the morality of an action is determined by 'the greatest good to the greatest number'.

Utilitarianism was proposed by David Hume (1711–76), but was first fully formulated by Jeremy Bentham (1748–1832) and then further elaborated by his student John Stuart Mill (1806–73). The idea that whether an action is right or wrong depends on whether it does more good overall than harm may not today seem particularly revolutionary, and may just sound like common sense. 'Who could argue,' as Rachels (1999: 98) observes, 'with the proposition that we should oppose suffering and promote happiness?' But he goes on to say:

> Yet in their own way Bentham and Mill were leading a revolution as radical as either of the other two great intellectual revolutions in the 19th century, those of Marx and Darwin. To understand the radicalness of the Principle of Utility, we have to appreciate what it leaves out of its picture of morality: Gone are all references to God or to abstract moral rules 'written in the heavens'. Morality is no longer to be understood as faithfulness to some divinely given code, or some set of inflexible rules. The point of morality is seen as the happiness of beings in this world, and nothing more; and we are permitted – even required – to do everything possible to promote that happiness.

Bentham also referred to 'the principle of utility' as 'the greatest happiness principle'. In determining whether an action had led, on balance, to greater general happiness, everyone should be counted alike and 'happiness' should be determined by reference to the presence of pleasure and the absence of pain. He thus promoted a variety of utilitarianism referred to as *hedonistic* (pleasure-based) *utilitarianism*. Other kinds of utilitarianism have been proposed, such as *preference utilitarianism* which tallies up the consequences of actions according to whether or not they meet our preferences rather than according to whether or not they give us pleasure.

Bentham also worked on the basis that the morality of *individual actions* could be determined by their consequences: a form of utilitarianism known as *act utilitarianism*. An alternative to this is *rule utilitarianism*, under which it is not individual actions but *general rules of conduct* that are judged according to whether they contribute to the greater happiness. Mill suggested that the principle of utility could be used to generate rules of conduct, and that the morality of individual actions could then be measured against those rules.

Rule utilitarianism versus act utilitarianism

The difference between rule utilitarianism, as against act utilitarianism can be illustrated by the example in Exercise 2.3. In our discussion of this exercise we gave two different utilitarian arguments (points 2 and 3 in our commentary). One said that torturing the captured terrorist was justified because his suffering would be outweighed by the positive consequences for his many would-be victims. The other argued that: *In this particular case, torturing the captured conspirator might prevent more suffering than it caused, but in the long run it would cause more suffering, because it would allow the principle to be established that torture could be used in some circumstances – and this would mean that torture would end up being used in more and more cases, to the long-term detriment of everyone.* The former is an act-utilitarian argument, the latter is a rule-utilitarian argument. It is not uncommon in social work to come across situations where a given course of action might seem to be best in terms of the immediate interests of those involved, but where it might create an unhelpful precedent which in the long run could do more harm than good.

You may notice how this talk of universal rules derived rationally from basic principles starts to sound rather like as echo of Kant's categorical imperative and it is interesting that in Mill's view there was no real difference between Kant's categorical imperative and utilitarianism. Perhaps he had a point. If you consider Kant's dictum 'Act only on that maxim whereby you can at the same time will that it become a universal law' you can see that, to determine whether a maxim should become a universal law, you would need to weigh up the good and bad consequences of its being universally applied.

Exercise 2.5

Write down some objections to utilitarianism as a way of deciding moral questions.

Comments on Exercise 2.5

One difficulty with utilitarianism lies in the idea that good and bad consequences of an action or a rule can somehow be 'aggregated' and then weighed in the balance to come up with a single measure. But surely there are some actions that are so repugnant that we would all agree that they should not happen, even if they result in huge benefits for thousands of people. For instance: would we tolerate using a real living child for painful and fatal medical experiments, even if it could be demonstrated that millions of other children's lives would be saved as a result?

However, it must be acknowledged that such calculations are in fact constantly being made all the time, implicitly if not explicitly. To give one instance: we have a road system that results in a weekly toll of road deaths. No doubt a drastic reduction in the speed limit would reduce that toll. But in effect society has decided that it will accept a certain level of road deaths for the sake of the convenience and economic benefits that come from faster traffic flow.

One other point that might be made about utilitarianism as a method of determining right and wrong is that, while in theory the benefits and costs to everyone should be counted equally, in practice the needs of some people are weighted differently from others. This is a point we will come back to shortly.

Virtue ethics

We do not wish to suggest that deontology and consequentialism are the only possible ways of looking at how we determine moral questions. Philosophers have proposed a number of approaches which we do not have the space to go into here. But one other way of looking at the question is provided by what is called 'virtue ethics'. This has a very venerable history, dating back at least to the Greek philosopher Aristotle, who died twenty-three centuries ago, and has enjoyed a revival of interest recently among philosophers (see for instance Crisp and Slote, 1997; Crisp, 1998). On this view, an action is the right thing to do, not because of some sort of calculation as to its consequences, or because it concurs with a 'duty', but because it is consistent with 'virtue'. 'Virtue' is a rather old-fashioned word but what is meant by it in this context is generally recognised qualities such as courage, honesty, kindness. Aristotle's view on virtue was that:

- a virtue is 'a character trait that a human being needs ... to flourish or live well' (Hursthouse, 1998: 23), and
- virtue consists in striking a sort of happy medium between extremes. Thus: *courage* is a virtue, *cowardice* is a vice resulting from lack of courage and *recklessness* is a vice resulting from an excess of courage.

From the point of view of virtue ethics, the right thing to do is that which is consistent with living life as fully as possible. Virtue ethics differs from deontological and consequentialist ethics in that it focuses not on actions, but on 'agents' – that is on the persons carrying out the actions.

For an argument in support of applying virtue ethics in a social work context, you could look at McBeath and Webb (2002: 1015). They argue that 'in a complex socio-political world, social work ethics needs to re-cast the moral duty of the social worker in terms of virtue ethics'. They suggest that the problem with consequentialist approaches is that one can seldom accurately predict the consequences of one's actions, while a deontological approach will tend to result in the mechanical performance of a list of 'duties' as opposed to the spontaneous exercise of judgement based on understanding and experience:

> ... what account of morality can be given if the link between means and ends is often weak precisely because social work is a contingent, non-linear task? How can a worker do 'good' if their world is inconsistent? What price 'universalizability' of morality under the complex indeterminate world of social work? (McBeath and Webb, 2002: 1018)

Virtue ethics seems to us to have real attractions as an alternative way of thinking about how to live one's life generally and how to be a 'good social worker' in particular. It surely is important for social workers not just to follow rules but to be courageous and kind and honest. (It is these sorts of personal quality that service users typically notice and value.) So we agree that virtue ethics does provide a useful additional strand to thinking about ethical questions. However, McBeath and Webb are guilty of caricaturing the nature of deontological and consequentialist positions in order to make their point. We cannot see that, in a professional context, virtue ethics can provide an alternative to thinking about the consequences of actions, or of having clearly defined duties. All the same, we agree that personal qualities are important in social work as well as 'correct' actions, and that social workers must cultivate those personal qualities.

The following exercise invites you to try and find arguments based on virtue ethics to bring to bear on the imaginary debate in Exercise 2.1.

Exercise 2.6

In Exercise 2.1 a team leader, Richard, made out a case for closing down a popular 'call-in surgery' in the Greytown team patch, in order to allow the team to concentrate its resources on dealing with a backlog of child protection work. Arguments for and against were made by three other members of the team and we suggested that these arguments fell into deontological or consequentialist categories.

Let us now imagine that *another* team member – Kim – argues in support of keeping the surgery open, but uses an argument based on virtue ethics. Danny also uses a virtue-based argument, but does so in favour of closing the office.

Can you think of arguments that Kim and Danny might use?

Comments on Exercise 2.6

This is one of the harder exercises in this book! But here are some suggestions:

Kim might argue that, if the team cuts back on supportive services in favour of concentrating solely on child protection work, 'we will deteriorate as social workers. We will become more punitive and suspicious and authoritarian. If we are to continue to be good, honest, caring social workers, we need to strike a balance between our investigatory, policing role and our supportive, helpful, listening role.'

So Kim is arguing for balance (which, in Aristotle's scheme, is the root of all virtues) and for the need to maintain the virtues of kindness, openness and humility.

As for Danny, well perhaps he could argue that 'If we keep the call-in going when there is child protection work left undone, then we are not being honest with ourselves. We claim that we are here first and foremost to protect children, and yet here we are saying that we will leave some children less well protected in order to allow us to carry on doing something that we find easier and less uncomfortable than child protection work.'

You may or may not agree with Danny that it is being dishonest to put the call-in in front of child protection work, but the point here is that, by basing his argument on the virtue of 'honesty' he, like Kim, is using the kind of argument that is associated with virtue ethics.

Values and politics

The discussion so far has ignored the political context in which a decision, such as the closure of the call-in surgery in Exercise 2.1, takes place. But it is important that we consider that context and see how it alters our perceptions.

Exercise 2.7

Suppose that there is yet another participant in the discussion in Exercise 2.1, whom we will call Betty.

Betty dismisses all the arguments that have been offered by the others. The situation has become a farce, she says. The team has legal obligations *both* to children at risk *and* to families of children in need, but is clearly not adequately funded to meet these obligations.

'We shouldn't be struggling with this,' she says. 'We should be passing this up to the top, stating clearly that this team is failing to meet its legal obligations and will continue to do so unless given additional resources. We should force the council to see that it must either makes a publicly accountable choice between child protection and family support, or it must resource the service properly. Otherwise we're just putting a fig-leaf over it for them.'

What would you say is different about Betty's argument from all the other arguments so far presented?

Comments on Exercise 2.7

There are doubtless many differences. What we would draw your attention to is this: Everyone else has discussed the precise rights and wrongs of the two alternative courses of action. But Betty suggests that all that is irrelevant, a red herring. What is important to Betty is being clear about whose decision this really is and being clear about what has made the decision necessary in the first place. In other words, in Betty's view, the rights and wrongs of closing the call-in office or keeping it open are not really the point. The crucial issue is the inadequate resources that are being put into the service and the fact that the service cannot meet its legal obligations to provide both protective and preventative services.

She is trying to move the argument away from the rights and wrongs of this particular issue to the structural and political questions that lie behind it.

The utilitarian view of morality, as we have just discussed, is that 'good' actions (or good rules of action in the case of 'rule utilitarianism') are those which are on the whole beneficial and 'bad' ones are those which on the whole are harmful. The theory is that actions or rules are to be measured by their effect on *everyone*, with the effects on each individual weighted equally. But we know that in any society there are some people who are powerful – and in a strong position to shape public opinion – and others who are not. It seems likely therefore that our ideas about what is right and what is wrong are shaped, whether consciously or unconsciously, by those in a position of power. In actual practice is it not likely to be the case that people are not counted equally and that the calculation of the greatest good is weighted in favour of the good of some people or groups of people, as opposed to others? If this is so then 'bad' actions will tend to come to mean 'harmful to those in powerful positions', while good actions will tend to come to mean 'beneficial to those in powerful positions'.

If you prefer to prefer to talk in terms of duties, essentially the same argument applies. The duties and principles that exist in any given society arguably reflect the interests of those in power. In our society, for instance, it is generally agreed that it is wrong to steal, and this makes it wrong to shoplift an item worth a few pence from a department store. And yet it is not considered wrong for a wealthy person to accumulate for his own personal use millions or billions of pounds which otherwise could be used to save hundreds or thousands of lives (for, after all, many thousands die across the world every year for want of food or simple medicines). This is the kind of line of thought that led the nineteenth-century anarchist Pierre-Joseph Proudhon, in a book published in 1840, to ask the question 'What is property?' and give his own answer, 'Property is theft!' (Proudhon, 1994: 14).

Consider how much more indulgent a view society takes of tax evasion – a crime of the relatively well-off – than it does of benefit fraud, a crime of the poor. Or how, in societies where formal power is mainly or entirely held by men, a much more serious view is taken of female adultery and promiscuity than of male adultery and promiscuity. (You can probably easily think of half a dozen negative, value-laden terms that can be used for women who 'sleep around' but it is difficult to think of even one such word that can be used for promiscuous men.) Or think of the way in which, in nineteenth-century America, atrocities committed by Native Americans against white people were taken as evidence of their 'savage' nature and unfitness to run their own affairs, but the many atrocities committed by white people against Native Americans were not taken as evidence of the savagery of *whites*, or of *their* unfitness to govern themselves. All these examples illustrate ways in which societal values are shaped by – and skewed in favour of – the interests of those in power. (More specifically they illustrate how societal values may be distorted by, respectively, *classism, sexism,* and *racism.*)

The classic formulation of the view that values, including morality, are the product of the power relations in a particular society, is that of Karl Marx (1818–83). In *The Communist Manifesto*, published in 1848, Marx and his collaborator Friedrich Engels rhetorically address the capitalist ruling class (the bourgeoisie) in the following terms:

> Your very ideas are but the outgrowth of bourgeois production and bourgeois property, just as your jurisprudence is but the will of your class made into a law for all, a will whose essential character and direction are determined by the economical conditions of existence of your class. (Marx and Engels, 1967: 101)

You do not have to subscribe to the whole philosophy of Marxism to see that societal values *are* likely to be shaped by the interests of the powerful and that there are serious implications for social work as a result. Social work is a profession that works with the least powerful groups in society. But social work's values and its terms of reference are given to it by the state and by society at large – and therefore, by those who have power.

The French thinker, Michel Foucault (1926–84) pointed out that what is accepted as 'true' varies from one historical period to another. As he put it, 'Every society has its own regime of truth, its "general politics" of truth: that is the types of discourse which it accepts and *makes function as true*' (Foucault, 1980: 131, our italics). What is accepted as 'true' is related to power. Those who are powerful are those who are able to dictate what is defined as 'true'. To illustrate this with a social work example, consider the different weight that might be given, in a courtroom for example, to, say, the views of a consultant psychiatrist who proposes a medical explanation for a given behaviour and a social worker who offers a purely social explanation. Which 'truth' prevails – the 'medical' or the 'social' explanation – may not be the result of the objective merits of either model but rather of the relative power of the speaker and the relative power of the world-view which he or she represents. In another context, a witch doctor, a priest or an astrologer might be the one whose version of 'truth' carried the day.

But of course, while a social worker's view may not always prevail against that of a psychiatrist, a social worker is often much more powerful that a social work service user and may well be able to impose her own 'truth' – her 'professional opinion' – over the 'truth' of a service user. It is therefore necessary for social workers to keep asking themselves the following uncomfortable question: *I may think I am doing the right thing and being helpful to my service users, but am I really being helpful to them, or am I actually contributing to their oppression?* Just because we think we are doing the right thing does not, unfortunately, necessarily mean that we really are.

The radical strand of thinking about social work responds to these kinds of concern by insisting on the need for a political commitment from social workers. Concepts such as *empowerment* and *anti-oppressive practice* have partly arisen as a result of awareness of the fact that social work can be, or is in danger of becoming, a tool to impose the values and the agenda of the powerful on the powerless. We return to these matters in Chapter 6.

Chapter summary

In this chapter we have dealt with:

- Values and ethics as philosophical problems
- The problem of relativism
- Deontological theories
- Consequentialist theories
- Virtue ethics
- Values and politics

We hope that this chapter will have convinced you that thinking about the origins of value systems is not just an intellectual game, but has practical implications.

Of course we do not suggest that scholarly debates about the relative merits of utilitarianism and deontology are a common occurrence in the normal working day of a social worker. Indeed we suspect that you could probably get through an entire career as a social worker without hearing either of these two words mentioned. But debates about what is the right thing to do *are* common – and, if you look under the surface of these debates, you will find differences of view, not only about what is right and wrong in a given situation, but about how you make these value decisions in general. Social workers do take deontological and utilitarian positions, even if they do not use those words, and do advocate various kinds of virtue ethics, even if they never mention Aristotle. Likewise, though they may never have heard of Foucault, social workers do notice the way that power shapes, and is shaped by, the way that we view things and what we perceive as 'right' and 'true'. And, whether or not they refer to Marx, any thoughtful social worker becomes aware that issues to do with social structures do often hide behind what may seem on the surface to be purely personal questions.

One thing that will have become clear from this chapter is that there is no single way of determining what constitutes 'right' and 'wrong', let alone of deciding what is right or wrong in a given instance. Many people, however, are guided by strongly held religious beliefs – and it is this that we consider in the next chapter.

3 Values and Religion

- Social work values and religion: historic links
- Recognising religious needs
- The multi-faith context
- Challenging religion
- Limits of the 'scientific' model
- Notes for practice

> Man lives in three dimensions: the somatic, the mental and the spiritual. The spiritual dimension cannot be ignored, for it is what makes us human. (Frankl, 1968, as cited in Loewenberg, 1988: ix)

Since this is a book on social work values and ethics, some readers may feel that the inclusion of a chapter specifically on religion is odd and perhaps irrelevant. We felt, though, that the book would have been incomplete without it because religious faith is undoubtedly one of the main sources from which people derive their systems of values (see Exercise 2.2). Indeed, as we have already noted in the previous chapter, most people in the world today would probably still identify one or other of the traditional religious faiths as the basis of their values. Many of the users of social work services certainly do so, and so too do many social workers. Indeed many of the founders of social work as a profession, and many of the oldest and most well-known social work agencies, had and still have a quite explicit religious base.

It is not our aim, of course, to promote any particular faith here. This would be impossible, for the two authors of this book have opposing views: Andrew is a practising Christian, Chris an atheist. We do both agree, however, that any serious discussion of the role of values in social work should open at least a window on to the role of religion or faith (we will use the words interchangeably) in people's lives. Social work is about meeting people's needs, and it cannot afford to ignore the fact that many people – even among those who are not religious in a formal sense – see 'spiritual needs' as being of central importance, or the fact that, for many, religion provides a means of meeting those spiritual needs. Indeed, as we will see, British law *requires* social workers to think about the religious needs of service users, and we suspect that similar requirements exist in other jurisdictions.

Exercise 3.1

Before going further, you may like to reflect on the following questions:

- What does religion mean to you? Do you subscribe to a particular religion? Were you brought up in one? What kinds of feelings do you have towards religion?
- How much would you say your beliefs about 'right' or 'wrong' are based upon religious teachings?
- How does your position on religion influence how you see others and the world we live in?
- How does it influence the way you see people who take a different view on religion to yourself?
- Do you find it difficult to talk about religion in a social work context? Would you want to?

Comments on Exercise 3.1

These are very personal questions. Any two individuals – even two individuals who work together well and would agree on many other things – can turn out to have radically different views on religious questions. The two authors of this book are a case in point. It is a curious fact that two people can disagree profoundly on the fundamental nature of the universe, and yet work together quite satisfactorily on the problems thrown up by everyday life. But it is fortunate that this is so, because in any society (and especially in a multicultural one) each of us is surrounded by people who disagree with us on these fundamental questions.

While people with fundamental differences in religious belief can work together, it may be challenging. For example, some religious people believe that only those who subscribe to their own faith will be saved from eternal punishment. To other people, this can sound pretty much like saying 'The rest of you can all go to hell' – and it can arouse strong negative feelings. Equally, some non-believers are inclined to laugh at religion and dismiss it as ignorant superstition on a par, say, with belief in Santa Claus or the tooth fairy. For religious people, whose beliefs and religious practices form a profoundly important part of their lives, this may feel extremely disrespectful and hurtful – and it can make people reluctant to bring up their religious views for fear of ridicule. Because of the potential for conflict and uncomfortable feelings, discussion of religious differences – and the religious dimension in people's lives – is very often avoided altogether.

Simply to avoid the topic in this way, though, does not seem to us legitimate for social workers, who have to deal with people with many different religious backgrounds.

Social work values and religion: historic links

Social work values and practices are rooted in traditions which derived from Christian, or Judaeo-Christian discourse. Although expressed today in language which has deliberately forgone its Christian tone, social work is built on assumptions about individual subjectivity, community and service to others which have a strong continuing presence in Christian discourse. (Cree, 1995: 50)

Cree suggests that the Christian tradition created the foundations upon which the modern social work profession's value base was laid. As a matter of historic record this is surely, at least in part, the case. Social work as a distinct profession developed primarily in Europe and North America, where Christianity is the dominant religious tradition, and many of the agencies which originally pioneered what we would now call social work were motivated quite specifically by Christian belief. Many of them still are: for instance, if we take three of the UK's largest independent providers of child welfare services: the Children's Society is an offshoot of the Church of England, the National Children's Home has Methodist roots and Barnardo's still quite explicitly states that it

... derives its inspiration and values from the Christian faith. Today we work in a multi-cultural society, but we are proud of the Christian values and beliefs upon which we were founded. (Barnado's website, May 2004)

Dr Barnardo himself is just one of a number of specifically Christian 'founding fathers' of what we would now recognise as social work, and there are many eminent 'founding mothers' too who were likewise motivated by their

Christian faith, among them Elizabeth Fry, Josephine Butler and Octavia Hill. Felix Biestek (1963), who is widely quoted in books on social work values and remains hugely influential, was a Roman Catholic priest. His code of ethics is rooted in a tradition of Christian ethics and theology, as much as in any philosophical tradition, and certainly does not owe its origins to the social sciences upon which social work has traditionally drawn for its intellectual base. Terry Philpot (1986) points out that Biestek's principle of respect for persons cannot be 'derived from the social sciences at all, but is, in essence, a religious value, having its justification in a transcendental view of life' (Philpot, 1986: 143). Clearly the social sciences *cannot* be expected to come up with answers to value questions, for (to repeat a quotation which we offered in Chapter 1) 'No amount of knowledge of what is the case can ever establish for us what we ought to do about it' (Downrie and Telfer, 1980: 22), although – as we saw in the previous chapter – many would argue that value systems can be built on other bases than religion.

Of the major religions Christianity is not the only one that has been influential in social work. There are long-standing Jewish social work agencies. In Islam, the obligation to give help to those in need is a fundamental tenet of the faith, with *zakaah* (or *zakat*), the giving of alms, being the third of the five 'pillars of Islam'. Buddhism has been an influence in social work thinking not only in predominantly Buddhist countries, but in Western countries too. (See for instance the work of our late colleague David Brandon, 1990, 2000, who was also interested in Taoism.) However, Christianity is almost certainly the most influential religion in the development of social work as a modern profession, perhaps because professional social work is something that emerged in the industrialised world and it was in the predominantly Christian West that the industrial revolution began. (The historical relationship between religion and social work in this country is well documented by the work of Philpot, 1986, and Cree, 1995.)

In view of the history and of the continuing links between religious faiths and social work agencies, it is interesting that talk about the relationship between social work and its Christian roots sometimes seems (in our experience) to create a certain unease in social work circles, as does talk about the 'spiritual' dimension of life generally. But even social workers who are confirmed atheists cannot avoid the fact that many of the roots of their own profession and its values go back to the Christian ethic of serving God through charity, an ethic which is shared by the other major religions. An atheist or humanist might wish to recast this ethic in terms that did not include the idea of a personal God – we might talk of empathy for others as being part of what it means to be human: a recognition of the fact that we are part of a greater whole – but the fact remains that many of the founders of social work would have cast it in its specifically religious form.

Recognising religious needs

> ### Religion
>
> Religion is defined by the *Concise Oxford English Dictionary*, 7th Edition, 1982 as a
>
> 1. particular system of faith and worship (the *Christian, Muslim, Buddhist* religion)
> 2. human recognition of superhuman controlling power esp. of a personal God or gods entitled to obedience and worship, effect of such recognition on conduct and mental attitude
> 3. thing that one is devoted to ...

Whether or not social workers are motivated by religious faith, there can be no doubt that many of the people they work with will be. For many people belief in 'a supernatural controlling power', and in an afterlife, meets an important need. There is even some empirical evidence to suggest that subscribing to a religion can have beneficial effects on mental health (Kalish and Reynolds, 1976, for instance, found that people who had strong religious convictions had less anxiety about death, though atheists did better than people with confused and unclear religious beliefs). For many, religion also provides a significant sense of *belonging*. Holding on to a particular faith, and its attendant practices, is a crucial part of their identity.

Failure to recognise the importance of religion in the lives of service users can, at worst, amount to an attack on their sense of well-being, their integrity and their identity. This is recognised in law in the UK and elsewhere. In England and Wales, the Children Act 1989, the NHS and Community Care Act 1990, and the Criminal Justice Act 1991 all make specific reference to the importance of religion in the provision of care. Thus, in Section 22 5(c) of the 1989 Children Act, the local authority is required to give 'due consideration ... to the child's religious persuasion, racial origin, cultural and linguistic background'. This requirement was reinforced by Department of Health guidance accompanying the Act. For example, when it comes to placement of children in foster care, local authorities are required 'to place a child, where possible, with a foster parent of the same religious persuasion as the child or with a foster parent who will undertake to bring the child up in that religious persuasion' (Department of Health, 1991: 33).

Exercise 3.2

Can you think of instances where failure to recognise the religious beliefs of a service user would result in basic needs going unmet?

Comments on Exercise 3.2

Here are two imaginary scenarios:

Mr Patel, an elderly Hindu man, is admitted to a residential home in an emergency, due to the hospitalisation of his carer. He is frightened and disorientated. All of the residents in the home are white British and the staff are either white British or black British of African-Caribbean origin. The staff in the home are proud of their cultural awareness and when it comes to meal-times, they inform Mr Patel that they have gone to some trouble to provide pork-free meals made using halal meat. Some of the care staff seem to think they have already gone some way beyond the call of duty to meet what they are inclined to see as pernickety dietary foibles. Sensing this, Mr Patel does not feel able to tell them that in fact he is a Hindu, not a Muslim, and that his faith prohibits the eating not of pork but of beef, as the cow is a sacred animal in Hinduism. Many Hindus are completely vegetarian, in fact, though Mr Patel is not. But to eat food which might include beef feels to Mr Patel like an act of self-pollution, degradation and wickedness. Already feeling frightened, lost and deprived of the familiar environment which normally gives his daily life some structure and meaning, Mr Patel feels he has no choice but to decline food altogether. What seems a minor matter to non-religious people may be for a religious person, a matter that goes deep to the core of their sense of self-worth and belonging.

Jane, aged 15, is a white British girl who has been temporarily accommodated away from her family in a foster home due to allegations made about a family member which suggest that she may be at risk at home. This is a very lonely and very frightening situation. Jane is an active member of an evangelical Christian church, and has derived a great deal of support both from the other members of the church and from the belief system which Christianity provides.

It is important to her at times of difficulty to be able to pray and to be able to turn to other church members. However, the social worker who placed her here has not picked up on this dimension in Jane's life. Jane has experience of being ridiculed by her peers for her religious beliefs and she has already heard her foster father (who is unaware of her religion) making disparaging comments about 'bible-bashers'. She is frightened to pray for fear of being discovered, and does not know how to go about asking to be allowed to contact her church. Jane is therefore cut off from sources of support which would help her through this difficult time.

The multi-faith context

Recognising and responding to religious needs is, of course, more challenging in a society in which many different religious traditions coexist. Social workers need to understand how different faiths, in very different ways, help in maintaining and supporting their communities. They need to understand some of the dynamics of these diverse communities and apply their understanding to their practice. Indeed the very nature of the relationship between an individual and a community is something that may vary in different communities. In the Western, secular context, the individual may be seen as paramount. In some other communities, the needs of the individual may come second to those of the community.

Thompson's (2001) PCS model may be helpful here. The model offers a straightforward frame for looking at how inequalities and discrimination manifest and perpetuate themselves in 'the social circumstances of clients, and in the interactions between clients and the welfare state'. The model operates on three levels: the P level (personal or psychological), the C level (the cultural level: 'shared ways of seeing, thinking and doing' Thompson, 2001: 21–3) and the S level that relates to structural matters.

Let us now apply this specifically to religion. Beginning with the P level and considering what religion can mean for individual people we can see that it can form the basis of some of the strongest emotions that people experience, and provide the underpinning for attitudes and thought patterns which may govern and direct the life of the believer and form the cement that sustains and holds that follower to a particular way of life. Religion can be a great source of strength and integrity though conversely, and as Thompson recognised, strong beliefs can also produce inflexibility that may lead to prejudice.

Moving to the C level, religion provides for many people a sense of shared belonging, a feeling of cohesion and membership of a family that unites believers and can, in some instances (though sadly not by any means in all) increase understanding or tolerance of the similar needs that are met by other faiths. In Islam, this community of believers is known as the *Ummah*, rather powerfully evoked in the following extract from a newspaper article:

> Ummah is sometimes defined as the community, sometimes the nation, sometimes the body of Muslim believers around the globe, and it has a physical reality, without parallel in any other religion, that is nowhere better expressed than in the five daily times of prayer.
>
> The observant believer turns to the Ka'aba in Mecca, which houses the great black meteorite said to be the remnant of the shrine given to Abraham by the angel Gabreel, and prostrates himself before Allah at Shorooq (sunrise), Zuhr (noon), Asr (mid-afternoon), Maghreb (sunset) and Isha (night). These times are calculated to the nearest minute, according to the believer's longitude and latitude, with the same astronomical precision required for sextant-navigation. (The crescent moon is the symbol of Islam for good reason: the Islamic calendar, with its dates for events like the Haj and Ramadan, is lunar, not solar.) Prayer times are published in local newspapers and can be found online, and for believers far from the nearest mosque, a $25 Azan clock can be programmed to do the job of the muezzin. So, as the world turns, the entire Ummah goes down on its knees in a never-ending wave of synchronised prayer, and the believers can be seen as the moving parts of a universal Islamic chronometer. (Raban, 2003)

A similar sense of belonging is key part of all religions. The Christian Bible, for instance, speaks of believers being 'one, as thou, Father, art in me, and I in thee, that they also may be one in us' (John 17: 21).

Finally, at the S level we can see many instances of organised religion being actively involved in striving to correct structural injustices (religious leaders were prominent both in the nineteenth-century campaign against slavery and in the twentieth-century struggle against apartheid, for instance) and in organised efforts to obviate the effects of oppression and discrimination. But we can also see ways that religion at this level can in itself be used for oppressive purposes (consider the oppression of women in the name of Islam in Afghanistan under the Taliban, or the torture and killings carried out in the name of Christianity by the Spanish Inquisition).

But it is the *interplay* of these three levels that is particularly subtle and complex. For instance a specific set of religious beliefs may meet real needs both for a community and for individuals within that community, and yet at the same time perpetrate oppression at a structural level. Religious beliefs may simultaneously be both liberating and oppressive.

In Europe and North America – and other parts of the world whose culture is European in origin – social work is typically an adjunct of a secular state whose laws, moral norms and customs are influenced both directly and indirectly by a Christian tradition and Christian values. These values are still ingrained in society, in the way that people live, think and behave, even if to a lesser extent today than formerly. With the increased multi-faith nature of these formerly Christian societies, however, there are likely to be tensions between the broadly speaking Christian values and structures that underpin society and the belief systems of other individuals and groups.

A competent social worker needs to be able to communicate with people who have very different beliefs about the world and, as Canda puts it, 'if students are not enabled to deal with religious value differences within the confines of a classroom; they will not be prepared to deal with them in the field' (1989: 38). Canda proposes a comparative framework for looking at issues of religion in social work education. He offers six points, which he believes social work education should follow:

- Examine religion and spirituality as a general aspect of human culture and experience
- Compare and contrast diverse religious behaviours and beliefs
- Avoid sectarian and anti-religious biases
- Encourage dialogue that is explicit about values issues and respect values differences
- Examine the potential benefit or harm of religious beliefs and practices
- Emphasise the relevance of social workers' understanding of religion to providing effective service to clients. (Canda 1989: 38–9)

Challenging religion

But if it is important to respect religious beliefs, it is equally important to recognise that respect for religious belief should not be uncritical and cannot override all other factors in a given situation. There is a necessary tension between the need to recognise the importance of religion to people – including religions whose basic tenets we ourselves may not agree with – while still retaining a willingness to challenge where necessary. It is in striking this balance in the real world that difficulties start to appear. If respecting other people's value systems is part of our own value system, then what do we do in situations where other people's deeply held beliefs lead them to behave in ways which, within the frame of our own value system, are simply wrong? This is not so much of a problem when those involved are, so to speak, 'consenting adults', but it becomes a real dilemma where there are children involved or other people who may not be in a position to make their own choices.

For instance both Islam and Judaism prescribe male circumcision – the removal of the foreskin of small boys – and this remains legal in the UK and other countries. In other circumstances taking a knife to a small child and removing a part of the body without a medical reason would be seen as a serious assault, which would occasion intervention by child protection services. But here is an instance where respect for religious belief is generally accepted as 'trumping' the need to protect children from violence, for circumcision in both traditions is an crucial marker of belonging and, even if we are not Muslims or Jews, we know that belonging – a sense of identity – is a basic human need. However, the question then arises as to where the limits lie to what is acceptable in the name of religion. In the UK and elsewhere, the much more drastic procedure of *female* genital mutilation, for instance, is not legal, even though it is also accepted as normal and appropriate in many parts of the world, and could itself be claimed as a marker of identity and belonging.

In the case of Victoria Climbié (Laming, 2003), who died in London in February 2000 at the hands of her great-aunt Marie-Therese Kouao and her partner, religious belief played a destructive role. British readers will almost certainly be familiar with this high-profile case which has led to much heart searching within British society, but briefly the circumstances are that Victoria was a child from the Ivory Coast in West Africa who was sent by her parents to live with her aunt, first in France and then in London, in order to get a good education. A good education was never provided. Instead Victoria was subjected to an appalling catalogue of cruelty leading to her death at the age of eight. Among the horrors to which she was subjected was being kept tied up in a black plastic bag containing her own excrement in an empty bath, while being forced to eat cold food placed in front of her on a piece of plastic.

Victoria's carers, we are informed in Chapter 3 of the Laming report (Laming, 2003), sought advice and guidance from churches as to how to deal with Victoria:

> ... On 29 August 1999, Kouao and Victoria attended the Mission Ensemble pour Christ ...
>
> The pastor here was Pascal Orome ... Kouao told him about Victoria's incontinence and he formed the view that she was possessed by an evil spirit. He advised that the problem could be solved by prayer.
>
> Two weeks after her first visit to his church, Kouao phoned Pastor Orome and told him that, following a brief improvement, Victoria's incontinence had returned. He claimed he reproached her for being insufficiently vigilant and allowing the spirit to return. (Laming, 2003: 32)

Later, shortly before her death, Kouao took Victoria to a church again:

> There is evidence to suggest that by 19 February 2000, Victoria was very ill. On this day, which was a Saturday, Kouao took her to the Universal Church of the Kingdom of God ... Audrey Hartley-Martin, who was assisting Pastor

Alvaro Lima in the administration of the 3 pm service, noticed the two of them coming up the stairs. They were shouting at each other and Victoria seemed to be having difficulty walking.

Kouao and Victoria were disturbing the service, so Ms Hartley-Martin took Victoria downstairs to the crèche. She noticed Victoria was shivering and asked if she was cold. Victoria replied that she was not cold but she was hungry. Ms Hartley-Martin obtained some biscuits for her ... she did not seek to ensure Victoria received any medical attention because she 'was not aware that the child was ill.'

At the end of the service, Pastor Lima spoke to Kouao about the difficulties she said she was having with Victoria, particularly her incontinence. He expressed the view that Victoria's problems were due to her possession by an evil spirit and said he would spend the week fasting on Victoria's behalf. He believes he made it clear that Victoria was not expected to fast herself ... (Laming, 2003: 35)

These churches were only two out of many different bodies which failed to recognise the seriousness of Victoria's plight. However, by constructing Victoria's problems as something within herself – 'possession by an evil spirit' – they were profoundly unhelpful. Firstly, it seems likely that by allowing her aunt to see Victoria as a person possessed by an evil spirit (rather than as a very unhappy little girl – and latterly as a very ill little girl) the church inadvertently helped to legitimise the catalogue of physical abuse and mental cruelty to which she was subjected. Secondly, blinded by their own 'spiritual' explanations for what was happening, the churches failed to see what was really going on, until it was too late. When Kouao reported that Victoria had been unconscious for two days and had neither eaten nor drunk anything, Pastor Lima did eventually advise that she should go to hospital. She was admitted to the North Middlesex Hospital and then moved to St Mary's Hospital Paddington, where, in spite of medical intervention, she was to die, suffering from severe hypothermia and multi-system failure, with injuries so extensive that one doctor said they were 'too numerous' to record.

Exercise 3.3

Thinking about the involvement of the churches in the Victoria Climbié case, what general lessons do you think social workers could draw about their response to explanations for events based on religious beliefs, and what dangers are there to be avoided?

Comments on Exercise 3.3

Among the lessons that we would draw from this story are that respect for other people's religious beliefs cannot be extended to the point of failing to challenge 'spiritual' explanations for events which seem to have other causes, or religious justifications for behaviour which would seem to be likely to cause harm. It is important to guard against the danger of failing to challenge for fear of offending religious sensibilities.

This is easy to say, but harder to put into practice. As we have already shown, using the case of male circumcision as an illustration, even behaviour and beliefs which, from the point of view of a non-believer, are harmful may need to be tolerated and accepted in recognition of a bigger picture in which these behaviours or beliefs provide benefits to the individuals involved as well as immediate harm. So, although there is a danger in failing to challenge, there is also the opposite danger of challenging practices and beliefs without understanding the wider context.

Clearly in the case of Victoria Climbié there was no wider context in this sense. There was no sense in which she could be said to have benefited from being seen as possessed by evil spirits. In a situation of this kind, the duty to protect vulnerable individuals from harm must take precedence over the duty to respect religious beliefs.

In the long run what seems to be needed too is for professional agencies to build links with churches and other religious organisations, both at the local level and at a structural level, so that there is more trust and more understanding of each other's perspectives. As we have seen, Pastor Lima did eventually take steps to get Victoria to hospital, but it was too late. Perhaps if he had had better links with local professional agencies, he would have felt to able to involve them at an earlier stage.

Limits of the 'scientific' model

A social work curriculum that deletes or omits content related to the spiritual dimension may be called 'hollow'. (Sollod, 1992: A60)

Having criticised the churches in the Victoria Climbié case for allowing themselves to be blinded by 'spiritual' explanations, it seems appropriate to balance this by noting that the 'spiritual' dimension is important in thinking about human life, and that it is possible too to be 'blinded by science'.

In the second half of the twentieth century, social work came increasingly under the influence of models of human behaviour derived from the social sciences, which offer explanations for human behaviour in terms which emulate those of the natural sciences. Freudian psychology and its various offshoots is one example. Psychodynamic theories emulate the physical sciences by attempting to explain human behaviour in terms of a dynamic interaction of forces. Behaviourism is another example, as is, in its way, Marxism. These may seem very different to one another, but what they do have in common is a degree of determinism: the assumption that a person is the product of circumstances and that we can explain why a person behaves in a given way in terms of various mechanisms, rather in the way that (say) an astronomer can explain the movements of planets and stars by calculating the interplay of momentum and gravitational forces, or a chemist can explain the properties of different substances in terms of the properties of atoms and molecules. It can be useful to look at things in this way and it is certainly not our intention here to discredit the social sciences, though none of the three approaches mentioned has anything *like* the same predictive precision that can be achieved in chemistry or astronomy.

What we want to note, though, is that this way of looking at people is necessarily a *partial* view. There is a danger, if we only look at things in this 'scientific' way, that we will begin to see the users of our services as mere passive recipients of 'help', with the social worker, alongside other practitioners of the human sciences, as a technocratic expert whose job it is to 'fix' defective lives as a mechanic fixes defective engines. This is not an appropriate model for at least two reasons. Firstly, as we have already noted, it is inappropriate because nothing like this level of expertise exists in the human sciences, where the ability to predict and explain is at best limited, and where theories and models are almost all matters of discussion and dispute. Secondly it is demeaning to the users of services to view them as the products of their environment and history rather than as the free agents that we assume ourselves to be.

Even some of the more 'radical' and less 'scientific' modern formulations of the social work role may be guilty of this tendency to deny agency to service users if they construct users of social work services merely as victims of social injustices and misfortunes of various kinds, without balancing this with a view of service users as moral beings making their own moral choices. There is a germ of truth in the tabloid stereotype of the social worker as a person who makes excuses for bad behaviour. (The magazine *Punch* once printed a cartoon of Genghis Khan riding out to pillage and slaughter with an earnest social worker on the horse behind him, all ready to explain away his actions in terms of childhood trauma and a broken home.)

There is surely a point at which attempting to understand the reasons for someone's actions crosses over into denying to them the right to take responsibility for themselves. One of us has noted elsewhere, for instance, that if we accept that some residential social workers may be guilty of the crime of abusing children in their care, then we must also accept that some former care residents may be guilty of the crime of making false allegations of abuse. To suggest that only *we* are capable of evil and that service users are only capable of being *victims* of evil is, in a curious way, demeaning and oppressive (Beckett, 2002).

But science and, by extension, social science are necessarily in the business of *explanations*, which is why they are not of much help with value questions and can obscure the fact that, as a matter of practical necessity, human beings must see themselves as making their own choices as they move through life. Holland observes that, while the profession

> has drawn heavily upon various theories of human development, it has paid little attention to the processes and contents of the moral and spiritual dimensions of human experience. Too often we have examined human relationships and social issues not as moral and spiritual issues, but rather as technical matters to be understood in terms of refined psycho-social theory and empirical research. (Holland, 1989: 35)

While it is important to look for explanations – and to recognise that human beings are in a sense products of their environment – it is also important to simultaneously hold in mind a view of people as free to make choices. And for such a perspective we have to look elsewhere than the social sciences. There are a number of places we could look for alternative models. We could look at existentialist philosophy, for instance, or at Carl Rogers's person-centred therapy (Rogers, 1967). But another place to look is in any one of the major religious traditions, all of which have for centuries constructed the human individual as an active agent, a moral being, making choices between good and evil, right and wrong. We return to this theme in Chapter 7.

Notes for practice

We will conclude this chapter with a few brief notes on good practice with reference to religious belief.

- Developing a genuinely comprehensive picture of people, their needs and their strengths must include consideration of the role that religious or other belief systems play in their lives. The picture would be seriously incomplete without such consideration and it would be contrary to the basic principle of respect, which we discuss further in Chapter 8, to attempt an assessment without looking at what is important to the service user, or how the service user sees and interprets the world.

- In practice this requires that social workers make it their business to acquire a working knowledge of different religious traditions, as and when they encounter them. Of course it also requires recognition that religion is not homogeneous: the beliefs of one Christian are not necessarily the same as the beliefs of another Christian, the beliefs of one Muslim not necessarily those of every Muslim. And many people have idiosyncratic beliefs and value systems which cannot be neatly pigeonholed into the categories of established religious faiths.
- Failure to recognise the religious dimension in people's lives can not only result in important needs going unmet. It can also result in behaviour being misinterpreted. Andrew is reminded of a story about a black woman who was thought to be schizophrenic because she was speaking apparent gibberish into thin air. In actual fact, the woman was praying in a dialect that was unfamiliar to the psychiatrist and those carrying out the assessment.
- Regardless of whether or not we share a person's religious beliefs, or find those beliefs personally convincing or appealing, we must recognise that such beliefs are for many people the bedrock on which they construct meaning and purpose in their lives, and the means by which they make sense of value questions (the very kind of question which this book explores).
- But this is not to say that an uncritical acceptance of all beliefs and practices prescribed by different religions is required. As we have demonstrated that there are circumstances in which other factors must take priority.

Chapter summary

In this chapter we have considered the role that religion has played as a source of meaning and a reference point for value questions, both in life generally, and in social work in particular. The topics covered have been:

- Social work values and religion: historic links
- Recognising religious needs
- The multi-faith context
- Challenging religion
- Limits of the 'scientific' model
- Notes for practice

This concludes Part I, which has taken a fairly broad look at 'values'. Part II will focus more closely on the social work context, beginning in Chapter 4 with a consideration of the meaning of 'professionalism' in that context.

PART II

Values and
Social Work

4 The Professional Context

- Values at work
- What is a profession?
- Professionalism
- Professional ethics
- Codes of practice for social work
- Social work values
- Real world dilemmas
- Social work paradoxes

In Part II of this book, we will look more closely at values in the specific context of social work as a professional activity. In the next three chapters we will look at what sorts of values are – or should be – the basis of 'professional' practice in general and of social work practice in particular. And we will consider the difficulties that exist in actually applying those values in the real-world context of competing pressures and other agendas, hidden or explicit. This chapter provides an overview of this topic and considers 'professionalism' as a value. The next chapter will look at the dilemmas that arise from the fact of finite resources in social work agencies. Chapter 6 will consider the additional layers of ethical questions that are raised by the unequal power relationship that exists between social work, its employers and its users and recipients.

Values at work

As we said in Chapter 1, our values, and the values of the society around us, inform the choices we make not just at work but in every area of life. But there are several important ways in which a working context is different from other contexts in which we act and make choices. The rules of conduct, often unwritten, which we apply in everyday life are not necessarily sufficient to cover our conduct at work for reasons which include the following:

- Some pieces of behaviour which might be perfectly acceptable in a non-work context may not be acceptable in a work context. It is not regarded as acceptable, for instance, for a doctor to enter into a sexual or romantic relationship with a patient, even if both the doctor and the patient are single adults.
- Conversely, in a professional role, we may need to behave in ways that fall outside what would be acceptable in everyday life. Surgeons cut people open. Lawyers present arguments which they do not necessarily agree with. 'Approved social workers' in England and Wales, under the 1983 Mental Health Act, make decisions which can result in people being detained against their will.
- When we are at work we are not just there to be ourselves, we are there to perform a certain role for the benefit of others (whether they are called patients, customers, clients, pupils, students or service users) who need to know what to expect from us in terms of what we can offer and standards of conduct (see Exercise 4.1 below).
- In the case of the vast majority of social workers when we are at work we are there to perform certain functions on behalf of our employers. We are not there just to do as we think fit, but to fulfil our contract with our employers. (As we will see, this is not necessarily the case for other professions. Lawyers may be self-employed, either on their own, or as part of a partnership. Doctors in the UK *may* be employees of the National Health Service or of independent agencies, but they may be self-employed partners who contract their services wholly or partly to the NHS.)

In a working context it is necessary, for all these reasons, to have certain agreed standards of behaviour. Some of these may be specific to a particular employment contract. Some may be more general and take the form of standards which are supposed to apply across a whole profession: a code of *professional ethics*.

Before going on, you might like to consider this from the perspective of a user of services.

Exercise 4.1

When you visit your doctor what expectations would you have of him or her in terms of standards of conduct? How do these expectations differ from those that you would have of a friend?

Comments on Exercise 4.1

Here are some that occur to us:

- You would expect your doctor not to pass on information to others without your express permission. With a friend you would probably work on the assumption that it was all right to pass on your news unless you made it clear that you did not want this to happen.
- You would expect doctors to keep themselves up to date on the topics which you come to see them about and to possess and maintain a certain level of skill and knowledge about the recognition and treatment of illnesses and other physical problems.
- You would expect your doctor – even if of the opposite sex – to be able, if necessary, to examine intimate parts of your body without making you feel that the encounter was in any way a sexual one, or one that would alter the nature of your relationship with the doctor. Very different expectations would apply in the case of a friend of the opposite sex.
- You would not expect the above standards of behaviour to require individual negotiation. So, for instance, in the event that you had to see another doctor in the absence of your own, you would expect the same standards to be adhered to.

To come at the same question in another way, the following exercise offers some examples of situations in which (we think) a social worker inappropriately crosses the boundary of her professional role:

Exercise 4.2

If you agree with us that the social workers in the following examples have behaved inappropriately, how would you describe the social worker's mistake in each case?

(Continued)

Exercise 4.2   (Continued)

(a)   The social worker for a 10-year-old boy, David, has established a very good working relationship with him. When she leaves her job to take up a new job elsewhere she promises always to keep in touch with him.

(b)   A social worker informs a disabled man, Arthur, that she has not been able to obtain for him a service that he had requested and that she had agreed was appropriate to his needs. 'If I was in charge you would get it, Arthur,' she says, 'but unfortunately my managers only seem to think about money.'

(c)   A 15-year-old girl, Lisa, hints that she has been sexually abused. Her social worker encourages her to talk, telling her that 'It's safe to tell me anything you want. I'm just here to listen to whatever you want to say.'

(d)   An Approved Social Worker signs an application for a woman called Judy to be detained in a mental hospital under Section 2 of the 1983 Mental Health Act. The social worker doesn't think the legal grounds have been strictly met (Judy has been diagnosed as suffering from a mental illness, but there isn't really any evidence that Judy is a serious risk to herself or others), but the social worker decides to sign anyway because she believes that admission to hospital for assessment would be in Judy's best interests.

Comments on Exercise 4.2

(a)   It is extremely important not to make promises you can't keep to children, particularly to children who already have reason not to trust the adult world. Will this social worker really be arranging her life in ten years' time so she can keep in touch with David? Will it really be in David's interests to maintain contact with his former social worker when he needs to build a working relationship with his new social worker? This social worker is muddying the boundary between professional and friend.

(b)   Arthur will be disappointed and perhaps angered by the decision and the social worker is trying to avoid being the focus of that anger by blaming her managers. Is it really fair to say her managers are only interested in money? If she was a manager herself would she not also have to try and keep within the budget? This social worker is attempting to redraw the boundary between the agency and the service user in such a way that she places herself outside of it with the service user. But since she is in fact part of the agency this is fundamentally dishonest.

(c) It actually isn't safe for Lisa to tell the social worker anything – or not in the way that Lisa is likely to understand it. At least in the UK context, if Lisa discloses serious abuse, the social worker will be obliged to activate child protection procedures. This could result in a number of consequences which Lisa might well not want. It might lead to the break-up of Lisa's family, since the alleged abuser is likely to be arrested and could be charged and sent to prison. In some circumstances it might result in Lisa and other children in the family being taken into care. What happens once she has spoken will be outside Lisa's control and also outside the social worker's control. The social worker is therefore seriously misleading Lisa as to the boundaries within which she is operating.

(d) Here the social worker is acting illegally and is overriding another person's rights. She is taking it on herself to set aside the safeguards in the law which set limits to the circumstances under which people can be detained against their will.

What is a profession?

What do we mean by a 'profession' and by a 'professional'? Both words are used in a number of different senses. Most people would agree, for instance, that medicine and the law are 'professions'. Probably most people would not normally describe bricklaying or carpentry as professions, though no one would dispute that they involve skill and can be done in a 'professional' or 'unprofessional' way. The word profession has a narrow meaning and a broader one. 'Doing a professional job', and 'he/she is a real professional' are words of praise in all kinds of contexts. The narrower meaning of the word 'profession' is used in connection with certain specific occupations.

What defines a profession in the narrow sense? Among the characteristics associated with traditional established professions – professions in the narrow sense, like law and medicine - is that they require special training and specific skills and knowledge and that they are to quite a large extent self-regulating. Historically they have defined themselves and set their own standards of entry. To this day, for these professions, the bodies which set the standards of conduct and training consist of – and are largely controlled by – members of the profession itself.

Thus, for instance, in the UK the regulatory body for the medical profession, the General Medical Council states on its website (www.gmc-uk.org) that: 'We are not here to protect the medical profession – their interests are protected by others.' Nevertheless its 104-member council includes 79 doctors – 54 of them elected by doctors registered by the GMC and 24 appointed by educational bodies. It only includes 25 members of the public, who are appointed by the Privy Council.

In the UK, the legal profession is divided into two distinct groups – barristers and solicitors – each with its own regulatory system. The regulatory body for barristers in England and Wales is the Bar Council. It is made up of 115 barristers 'who are elected or represent the Circuits and Specialist Bar Associations', as its website states, and simultaneously with being the regulatory body, it is also the body which represents barristers' point of view:

> The Bar Council® is the regulatory *and* representative body for barristers and England and Wales [our italics]. It deals with the qualification and conduct rules governing barristers and those wishing to become barristers. It deals with complaints against barristers. It also puts the Bar's view on matters of concern about the legal system and acts as a source of information about the Bar. (www.barcouncil.org.uk)

For solicitors the Law Society provides the same dual function. It has a council of 105 seats of which 100 seats are allocated to solicitors elected by the membership and just 5 seats are allocated to lay members (www. lawsoc.org.uk).

By contrast, consider the new regulatory body for social work and social care in England, the General Social Care Council, set up in October 2001, which 'has responsibility for agreeing and issuing statutory codes of conduct and practice, setting up a register of social care workers, dealing with matters of conduct and regulating and supporting social work education and training' (www.gscc.org.uk/about.htm). It has nine lay members and eight professional members, none of whom are elected by the people that the Council regulates. All the members of the Council are appointed by the government in the person of the Secretary of State for Health (Care Standards Act, 2000, schedule 1, s 5). The chair must, by law, be one of the lay members.

Exercise 4.3

The two regulatory bodies for the law profession consist entirely or almost entirely of lawyers elected by lawyers. The medical regulatory body consists of more than 75 per cent doctors, of whom the majority are elected by doctors. The regulatory body for social care, by contrast,

---

Exercise 4.3   (Continued)

consists of less than 50 per cent social care professionals and is entirely appointed by the government.

Why do you think that law and medicine are largely self-regulating as professions, but social work and social care are not?

(Note that, while the GSCC regulates social work and social care in general, this book and the following discussion focus in particular on social *work*.)

Comments on Exercise 4.3

You may have come up with a number of possible reasons:

1   Medicine and law are more powerful and prestigious professions than social work. (You may like to consider why this is so.)
2   Medicine and law are professions that have been in existence for hundreds of years and their professional institutions have developed the way they have for historical reasons.
3   Medicine and law are professions which draw on a more specialist and distinct knowledge base than social work.
4   Another important difference is that medicine and the law are professions that are not dependent on the state or indeed on any other kind of institutional employer.

The last point, it seems to us, is important, and is not always remembered when the present and future state of social work is being discussed. People will always have reasons for seeking out the services of doctors and lawyers and will pay for these services themselves if necessary. Doctors and lawyers therefore do not need to work for anyone other than their clients/patients (even though, at the present time, it so happens that most doctors in Britain work for the state, whether as employees or as self-employed contractors, and many lawyers have part of their work paid for by the state through the Legal Aid system). We suggest that lawyers and doctors have, over the centuries, developed powerful traditions of self-regulation because from the outset they were separate from the state. The need to develop professional standards was a matter of self-interest, necessary if these professions were to win public trust, as much as it was a matter of public policy.

It is true also of, for instance, accountants and teachers that, in the absence of the state or institutional employers, their services would still be in demand. It is however *not* true of social workers in the same way. Although activities which we might recognise as social work (finding homes for unparented children, arranging care for people discharged from hospital) have gone on for hundreds of years they have always taken place under the auspices of the state or of other collective bodies such as churches or voluntary organisations. In the absence of these institutional employers, social work as a distinct occupation would not exist. Some people might employ the services of social workers privately, but in this case the social workers would become indistinguishable from counsellors or therapists. The nature of social work is such that most people who receive social work services would not be able to employ social workers privately, and some would not even want to – for many recipients of social work services have not themselves chosen to receive such services.

In short, leaving aside the historical differences, the differences in power and prestige and the differences in the kinds of knowledge base involved in each case, there is one fundamental difference between the legal and medical professions, on the one hand, and social work on the other. Medicine and law are not the creations of public policy, although of course they have to respond to public policy. But social work exists only as a result of public policy or public concern:

> all social work, to count as such, is authorised and legitimated as a result of public and political processes ... this remains true even in those regimes where the delivery of social work services is delegated to non-state organisations. (Clark, 2000: 4)

This does not mean that social work is not entitled to call itself a profession. It is difficult, demanding work which requires at least as high a level of skill (if it is to be performed well) as do law and medicine. But social work is not a profession *in the same way* that medicine and the law are professions. As Michael Horne emphasises, social work necessarily has 'interests and obligations ... other than those to the clients themselves' (Horne, 1999: 70).

Professionalism

Although bricklaying and plumbing are not generally described as professions (the word 'trade' is more commonly used), we do speak of bricklayers and plumbers performing a 'professional job' if the work is done skilfully and conscientiously. Professionalism in this sense is clearly to be admired and emulated. Lack of professionalism is to be criticised and avoided. So the word 'professional' is a value word when used in this way, meaning 'competent', 'thorough', 'skilful'.

But we use the word 'professional' – and its opposite 'unprofessional' – in a more specific way when we speak of 'unprofessional conduct' or say that 'X acted in a thoroughly professional way'.

Exercise 4.4

Think of instances of behaviour on the part of a social worker – or another professional such as a doctor – which you would regard as unprofessional. What does 'unprofessional' mean? What do we mean by 'acting in a professional way'?

Comments on Exercise 4.4

The sorts of things that you have thought of may have included:

- gossiping about information given in confidence;
- showing favouritism;
- entering into a sexual relationship with a service user or patient;
- basing decisions on whether you liked or disliked a person rather than on their needs;
- using your position to sell something to a service user or patient;
- using your position to pressure or coerce a service user or patient into doing something for you.

Why we regard all these behaviours as unprofessional is surely that they involve the person concerned stepping outside their assigned professional role in order to meet needs of their own, or indulge their own personal preferences.

Behaving 'professionally' in this sense is not just about skill, or competence, or conscientiousness, but something more specific. It is about

(a) playing the role that you signed up to when you joined the profession, and
(b) setting aside your own personal feelings where they conflict with that role.

In just the same way we speak of soldiers being professional when they conscientiously perform a difficult role, in spite of the feelings of fear, horror, exhaustion and so on which might make their purely personal feelings incline them to run away or hide. The need to be professional in this sense is very important in social work too, for social work often places us in positions that set off very powerful emotional responses – fear, rage, pity, disgust, shame, embarrassment – which may make us inclined to behave in ways that will get us out of having to do things that we find difficult and distressing, even if they are necessary in the interests of service users.

It is very easy in social work to slip into behaviour which is *unprofessional* in this sense of the word. The following exercise looks at this.

Exercise 4.5

The following are examples of unprofessional behaviour which it is quite easy to fall into. Which of these behaviours do you think you yourself are most likely to be prone to? Can you think of other kinds of unprofessional behaviour which you might be vulnerable to?

- Spending too much time on a particular case because you find the company of a particular service user rewarding.
- Failing to challenge a service user, or 'watering down' difficult messages because you find the service user intimidating and wish to avoid making them angry.
- Failing to challenge a service user, or 'watering down' difficult messages because you feel sorry for the service user and do not want to upset them.
- Telling service users about your own problems, perhaps out of a desire to demonstrate that you too are human.
- Colluding with service users against your own agency.
- Allowing your judgement to be swayed by service users or other professionals you find powerful and intimidating.
- Promising more than you can really deliver out of a desire to prove your usefulness.
- Performing tasks for a service user that they could really do themselves, in order to win their gratitude.
- Acting in a punitive way towards service users whose behaviour you dislike.
- Acting in a punitive way towards service users who have been dismissive or critical of your work.
- Tolerating or condoning the unprofessional behaviour of others, in order to avoid making yourself unpopular.

> ## Comments on Exercise 4.5
>
> Between us, at one time or other, we have probably erred in our own practice as social workers in quite a few of these ways, and we believe this would be true to a greater or lesser extent of most social workers.
>
> One aspect of becoming a self-aware, reflective professional social worker, we would suggest, is being honest with oneself about one's weak points. It is important to notice your own vulnerabilities and the situations in which they become apparent.

Professional ethics

We have seen that the word 'professional', as applied to a piece of work, contains:

- the broad meaning of competently and conscientiously done ('The builder did a very professional job on my extension'), and
- the more specific meaning of a role performed according to agreed standards of conduct, regardless of the personal feelings of the individual involved.

Both meanings imply work that adheres to certain standards. If you look at the websites of the various professional bodies such as the British Medical Association (www.bma.org.uk) or the British Association of Social Workers (www.basw.co.uk) or at the sites of regulatory bodies already mentioned such as the GMC or the GSCC (the Bar Council and Law Society serving, as we have seen, as professional associations and regulatory bodies rolled into one) you will see that maintaining standards is a central preoccupation of these bodies. To give an another example from another profession, the following are what the Royal Institution of Chartered Surveyors (www.rics. org.uk) describes as its four main aims:

- To maintain the highest standards of **education and training**
- To protect consumers through strict **regulation of ethics and standards**
- To advise global organisations, such as governments and regional boards
- To publish market **information and research**

So for the Chartered Surveyors' professional body in the UK, 'standards' include standards of competence and standards of training, but also include *ethical* standards and this is characteristic of professional standards generally. In the box below is a list of duties for doctors produced by the General Medical Council (www.gmc-uk.org/standards/doad.htm) which forms part of a much lengthier document of guidance on good medical practice.

The duties of a doctor registered with the General Medical Council

Patients must be able to trust doctors with their lives and well-being. To justify that trust, we as a profession have a duty to maintain a good standard of practice and care and to show respect for human life. In particular as a doctor you must:

- make the care of your patient your first concern;
- treat every patient politely and considerately;
- respect patients' dignity and privacy;
- listen to patients and respect their views;
- give patients information in a way they can understand;
- respect the rights of patients to be fully involved in decisions about their care;
- keep your professional knowledge and skills up to date;
- recognise the limits of your professional competence;
- be honest and trustworthy;
- respect and protect confidential information;
- make sure that your personal beliefs do not prejudice your patients' care;
- act quickly to protect patients from risk if you have good reason to believe that you or a colleague may not be fit to practise;
- avoid abusing your position as a doctor; and
- work with colleagues in the ways that best serve patients' interests.

In all these matters you must never discriminate unfairly against your patients or colleagues. And you must always be prepared to justify your actions to them. www.gmc-uk.org/standards/doad.htm

---

Codes of practice for social work

In the UK codes of ethics have been produced for social workers by the British Association of Social Workers (BASW, 2002), while the GSCC has produced two 'Codes of Practice', published together: one for the employers of social care workers, one for social care workers (GSCC, 2002: available on the web at www.gscc.org.uk).

The BASW document takes the form of a booklet in four sections. The first section is an introductory paragraph. The second is a paragraph giving a definition of social work. The third, extending over six pages and headed 'Values and Principles', begins by setting out five basic 'values' to which it says social work is committed (see box) and then looking at these values one by one and drawing out from them a set of 'principles'. The fourth and longest section, extending over nine pages, is headed 'Ethical Practice' and aims to apply the values and principles set out in the previous section to 'the principal areas of social work practice.' (As we discussed in Chapter 1, terms like 'values', 'principles' and 'ethics' are not necessarily defined in precisely the same way by every writer, but you can see that BASW's Code makes a three-tier distinction between (a) 'values', (b) 'principles' and (c) specific guidelines on ethical conduct.)

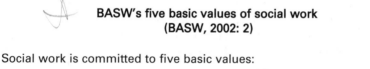

**BASW's five basic values of social work
(BASW, 2002: 2)**

Social work is committed to five basic values:

- Human dignity and worth
- Social justice
- Service to humanity
- Integrity
- Competence

Social work should both promote respect for **human dignity** and pursue **social justice,** through **service to humanity, integrity** and **competence.**

The American social workers organisation, the National Association of Social Workers (www.socialworkers.org) offers a strikingly similar list, with one extra core value added: 'the importance and worth of human relationships'.

**American social work values: The National Association
of Social Workers' 'core values'**

'The mission of the social work profession is rooted in a set of core values. These core values, embraced by social workers throughout the profession's history, are the foundation of social work's unique purpose and perspective

(Continued)

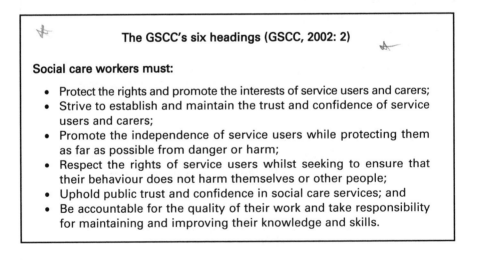

(Continued)

- service
- social justice
- dignity and worth of the person
- importance of human relationships
- integrity
- competence'

(From the preamble to the 'Code of Ethics of the National Association of Social Workers', as agreed by NASW's 1996 Delegate Assembly and revised by its 1999 Delegate Assembly: available from www.socialworkers.org)

Returning to the UK, and turning from the professional association of social workers to the government-appointed regulatory body, the GSCC Code of Practice for social care workers begins by setting out six points (they are not given a specific name such as 'values' or 'principles') under the heading 'Social care workers must ...' Each of these six points is then listed separately as a heading of its own with between four and seven bullet-pointed additional points. The six basic headings are listed in the box below.

The GSCC's six headings (GSCC, 2002: 2)

Social care workers must:

- Protect the rights and promote the interests of service users and carers;
- Strive to establish and maintain the trust and confidence of service users and carers;
- Promote the independence of service users while protecting them as far as possible from danger or harm;
- Respect the rights of service users whilst seeking to ensure that their behaviour does not harm themselves or other people;
- Uphold public trust and confidence in social care services; and
- Be accountable for the quality of their work and take responsibility for maintaining and improving their knowledge and skills.

These are two very different documents but they both purport to set standards for social work practice. It is worth taking a bit of time to compare the two texts:

Looking at the BASW 'Code of Ethics' and the GSCC 'Code of Practice', what differences do you notice between the two? Are they giving the same message? (You may find it interesting to compare them also with the GMC's 'duties of a doctor' which we cited earlier.)

Comments on Exercise 4.6

You have probably noticed other differences but one straightforward one is that the BASW guidance is for social workers while the GSCC guidance is for social care workers, a wider group of whom social workers are a subset. Possibly this explains some of the differences between the two documents. It is also worth noting that BASW is a membership organisation for social workers, while the GSCC is a government-appointed body with a majority of lay members.

Another difference is that the BASW document starts out from very broad, abstract 'values', while the GSCC launches into a list of things that social care workers should 'do'. The GSCC's code is more 'down to earth' and less idealistic in its tone and in this respect seems to bear more resemblance to the GMC's 'duties of a doctor'. An instance of this is that there is no specific mention of social justice in the GSCC code, while the BASW code includes social justice as one of its five key 'values.'

Social work values

The BASW Code assumes that the nature of social work can be summed up as certain core values which can generally be agreed to be 'social work values'. This is a widely held assumption. As Michael Horne remarks, '"Value talk" in social work often consists of lists of what it is considered the moral or ethical principles of social work are, or should be' (Horne, 1999: 1). He goes on to note that there are a number of competing lists (Timms, 1983; Butrym, 1976) but that 'there are generally strong similarities between them'.

Horne criticises an earlier version of the BASW Code of Ethics because 'it seems to ignore the important point that a set of ethical principles for social work should start with a consideration (or at least an acknowledgement) of the responsibilities of the social worker' (Horne, 1999: xiv). He points out that social workers are 'accountable to the authority of their employers (state or independent agencies) in the first place rather than to their clients for their decisions', a point that we discussed earlier when comparing social work with other professions.

In fact social workers are regularly in a position of having to take into account the interests of people other than their service users. This is the case, for example, when applying for a person to be detained in a mental hospital in order to protect the public (as already discussed, this is done, in England and Wales, by Approved Social Workers), or working with young offenders. In the consultation draft of the GSCC Code one of the six things that social care workers were supposed to 'do' was 'Balance the rights of service users and carers with the interests of society'. This was altered in the final draft to 'Respect the rights of service users whilst seeking to ensure that their behaviour does not harm themselves or other people'. The BASW Code states that 'in exceptional circumstances where the priority of the service user's interest is outweighed by the need to protect others or by legal requirements, [social workers will] make service users aware that their interests may be overridden' (BASW, 2002: 8). In both the codes as published there seems to be some reluctance to acknowledge that social workers do indeed often perform a balancing act between the rights of service users and the rights of others.

You may or may not agree, but again this serves to illustrate that the value base of social work is not necessarily something that there is universal agreement about (Nigel Parton and Patrick O'Byrne (2000: 37) have rightly referred to the 'contested and ambiguous nature' of social work). No one could dispute that values are central to social work - in some ways *uniquely* so for there are few purely technical questions in social work – but it does not necessarily follow from this that there exists a *single set of values* which all social workers can agree on.

However, we suggest that the following points are likely to be generally agreed:

- *Traditional professional ethics*
  As with the traditional professions, there is a need for social workers to adhere to a code of ethics which draws a clear line between their personal and professional lives and requires them to avoid abusing or misusing their position for personal ends. The 'duties of a doctor' cited earlier are a good summary of what these traditional professional ethics should consist of. Social work service users, like the patients of doctors and the clients of lawyers, are entitled to expect social workers to adhere to basic standards of competence and of integrity.

- *Social justice values*

    Social work value talk has always placed a strong emphasis on social justice. Of course, teachers, lawyers or doctors may be every bit as committed to social justice as social workers are, so it would be arrogant to claim a commitment to social justice as being in any way the exclusive province of social work. Nevertheless, because social work's particular specialism is in working with groups of people who are oppressed, discriminated against, or marginalised by society, it is particularly important that social work values should emphasise a commitment to social justice. At the very least social workers should make every effort not to *add* to the marginalisation and oppression of these groups. (Sadly, whatever its good intentions, adding to marginalisation and oppression is what social work does sometimes end up doing.) And, as far as possible, social work should not just avoid adding to oppression but should act in a way that promotes inclusion and empowerment. In Chapters 7, 8 and 9 of this book we will look in more detail at some of the implications of this, under the headings of 'Self-determination', 'Oppression and respect' and 'Difference and diversity'.

- *Respect for persons*

    Both traditional professional ethics *and* what we have called 'social justice values' seem to us to flow from the idea of respect for persons, which the BASW Code of Ethics expresses as 'human dignity and worth', and the American NASW Code expresses as 'dignity and worth of the person'.

- *Recognising our limits*

    One very important point made in the BASW code is that social workers have a duty to 'Recognise the limits of their competence...' (BASW, 2002: 7). Social workers are often under pressure to 'do something', but doing something is only ever justified if it is likely to improve things, since doing something in social work terms always involves an invasion of the privacy and autonomy of others. In the next chapter we will look at a related issue, the restrictions that are imposed by limited resources.

Earlier, in Exercise 4.1, we asked you to consider your expectations of your doctor in terms of standards of professional behaviour. A good test of your professional conduct as a social worker is to ask yourself how you would expect to be treated if on the receiving end of social work services and to check whether your own practice conforms to this. This is also a good test to apply to codes of professional conduct. Ask yourself the question: does this code set the standard that I personally would want to be met?

Exercise 4.7

Suppose that you are a parent and that, for some reason, a neighbour reports you to social services and says (incorrectly) that you are mistreating your child. What would you, as the subject of the referral, expect to happen?

Comments on Exercise 4.7

We do not know what your expectations would be. For ourselves, we would like:

- to know that the referral had been made;
- to be consulted before any other agencies were approached;
- to know precisely how the matter had been left, including what records were being kept on me and my child, and for how long, who had been informed about the referral and its outcome, and what had been said to them.

Malicious or unfounded referrals are a common occurrence and we know that in a busy social work office, a duty social worker, receiving a referral that she suspects may not be genuine, may be tempted to check with an agency such as a school that all is well with the child – and then close the case without taking any other action. The trouble with this is that, unknown to the family concerned, information about them (including an allegation of mistreatment) is now kept at the social work office and at the school. The parent or child has no opportunity to challenge the accuracy of any of it.

Genuine respect for persons surely entails treating other people as you would expect to be treated. But it is perhaps a little harder to decide how you would expect to be treated if you were behaving in a dangerous and irrational way.

Exercise 4.8

We hope that you never have the experience, but it is something that might happen to any of us. Suppose that you develop a psychotic

Exercise 4.8   (Continued)

illness or some other kind of delusional state which means that you become convinced that there is a world-wide conspiracy against you and your family. You believe that you can detect the people who are out to get you by 'listening to their thoughts' in the street. You decide that the best form of defence is attack and you inform your family that you intend to 'go after the enemy agents' and 'take them out by whatever means necessary'.

Neighbours contact the police and, as a result, community psychiatric services, including a social worker, become involved. This is in England and part of the social worker's task is to decide whether you should be detained under the 1983 Mental Health Act.

How would you, now, wish to be treated if this eventuality should occur in the future?

Comments on Exercise 4.8

We suspect that you would want to be prevented from doing something that you might regret for the rest of your life. Probably you would agree that physical restraint might have to be used to achieve this. The traditional social work value of 'respect for persons' is not always synonymous with allowing people to make their own decisions. Sometimes it is right to protect people against their own impulses.

But you would probably want the job to be done in a way that minimised the humiliation caused to you and ensured that, as far as you were able to understand, you were clear as to what was happening and what your rights were.

Probably you would also like to be sure that strong safeguards were built into the system used to detain you so as to prevent the misuse of this power.

Real world dilemmas

Codes of ethical conduct are easier to draw up than to apply consistently in practice. For one thing we are fallible human beings and there are all kinds of personal pressures that come to bear on us (in ways we explored in Exercise 4.4). For another thing social workers operate in organisations that are also fallible and human, where there are always political pressures to act in ways that do not necessarily constitute best practice (something that we will return to in Chapter 6). If your manager has a performance target to meet, for instance, she may be tempted to get you to do work that will help her to meet it, even if that work is not really the highest priority.

As we will discuss in Chapter 5, every social worker, too, inevitably has to operate with finite resources and a finite number of hours in the week, which means being forced into making difficult choices and compromises that you might prefer not to have to make. The duty social worker we mentioned in our comments on Exercise 4.7 might argue for example that if she took time to inform parents of the details of every such 'No further Action' referral – which we suggested was good practice – she would have less time to perform other equally important tasks.

But quite apart from all these pressures and limitations, the real world throws up ethical dilemmas: situations where values or ethical principles are placed in conflict with one another.

 Ethical Dilemma

'a choice between two equally unwelcome alternatives relating to human welfare...' (Banks, 2001: 7)

Ethical dilemmas of various kinds have been and will be discussed throughout this book. Here, for the present, are some examples of ethical dilemmas that are commonly encountered in social work, which we will then ask you to consider in Exercise 4.9:

1 Self-determination *versus* welfare (this arises in situations such as that described in Exercise 4.8).
2 Valuing cultural diversity *versus* protecting individuals.
3 The needs and wishes of a service user *versus* the needs and wishes of her carer.
4 Respecting confidentiality *versus* good inter-agency communication.
5 Self-determination *versus* the interests of the community.
6 The needs of communities *versus* the needs of individuals.

Exercise 4.9

Looking at the six examples we have just given of types of ethical dilemma that are commonly encountered in social work, try and think of examples of situations where these dilemmas might arise.

Comments on Exercise 4.9

The following are some suggestions, relating to various client groups. It should be possible to think of examples of dilemmas of these kinds arising in work with all client groups:

1   An adult man with a history of severe depressive illness insists, firmly and clearly, that he does not want treatment and does not want to enter a mental hospital. There is no reason to suppose he is a risk to others, but he has been getting increasingly depressed and has been increasingly expressing suicidal thoughts. He says people have a right to commit suicide if they wish. You are an Approved Social Worker trying to decide whether to apply for a section under the 1983 Mental Health Act.

2   A girl of Sudanese origin in the looked-after system (i.e. in pubic care) expresses a wish to visit relatives in Sudan, who are able to pay for her airfare. As her social worker, you are aware that in the community she comes from genital excision of girls (illegal in this country) is regarded as normal and proper and you suspect that the relatives intend to carry this out when she goes to Sudan.

3   A physically frail elderly woman depends on her married daughter for all her personal care. She cannot safely get out of bed by herself, cannot manage stairs, cannot bathe and cannot get out of the house. She refuses to have any other help in the home and is adamant that she will never consider entering residential care. Asked what she would do if her daughter would not help she says she would have to manage somehow. Her daughter is exhausted and her own health is suffering as a result of juggling the demands of her mother with the rest of her life.

4   Following a child abuse tragedy, agencies in your area have been criticised for poor communication. To improve communication

a local school sets up a system of 'Early Warning' meetings, to which social services, the police and local doctors and health visitors are invited, as well as social workers. At the meetings the school produces a list of children who are causing them concern and asks the other agencies to contribute what they know about these cases in order to build up a fuller picture and determine whether or not further action needs to be taken. You get to the meeting to find that a family you are working with is on the list. You know the family has serious marital problems and that the father is receiving treatment for alcoholism. What information do you share?

5 An eccentric elderly recluse lives in a house with no heating, running water or electricity with a large number of cats. He draws water from a well he has dug in the garden, which is otherwise completely overgrown. He is very dirty and with long filthy matted hair. He is verbally aggressive and will shout abuse and throw things at people passing in the street, but has never been known to actually harm anyone. Neighbours however say that 'something should be done about him' because he is frightening their children and causing a health risk.

6 You are a family social worker operating in an area of very high economic deprivation. A high percentage of families in the area are known to your agency because of concerns about child maltreatment, child behaviour and youth offending. Because of the community's experience of frequent intervention by social workers and frequent removals of children into public care, social workers are regarded with fear and suspicion in the area, as powerful agents of an oppressive state. How do you follow up (as you must) on new referrals about child maltreatment, without further contributing to this feeling of oppression and thus contributing to the general demoralisation and low self-esteem which is probably a factor in the high incidence of family problems?

Social work paradoxes

Every profession is faced with ethical dilemmas. Ethical dilemmas in medicine, in particular, are frequently in the news. But in some ways social work is unique because it is in a paradoxical position.

- On the one hand, more than any other profession, it traditionally identifies itself with those who are oppressed or marginalised by society. On the other hand it is created, sustained and funded by that same society, and largely by the state (in the UK even the profession's regulating body is, as we have seen, appointed entirely by the state).

- On the one hand social workers are encouraged to work in partnership with service users (e.g. Department of Health, 2000: 12). On the other hand, a large part of social work's brief – particularly in work with elderly people, mentally ill people and children and families – is to impose and police certain socially agreed norms, if necessary resorting to the law to compel compliance.

- On the one hand social workers are encouraged to be advocates for those they work with and to be guided by their needs (the needs-led assessment is central to the duties of social workers under the NHS and Community Care Act, 1990). On the other hand social work operates with finite resources and in practice social workers frequently have the task of informing service users that the services they want cannot be given. Indeed, within the state sector, one of the main functions of social work assessments is to gather information for the purposes of rationing.

At times social workers, like the members of the Greytown team in Chapter 2, may find themselves facing demands which are impossible to meet and may even be contradictory. At times, social workers may suspect that the role they are *really* being given to perform by society is different from the role which they are *ostensibly* being given.

Social workers, as we have discussed, have obligations both to their service users and to their employers, but these obligations do not necessarily pull in the same direction and may both pull in different directions to social workers' own needs and wishes as human beings.

Rules and codes are necessary and important in any profession, but being a good social worker is not, and never will be a matter just of following a set of rules, for the rules themselves are contentious. Ethical social work practice involves a difficult balancing act between competing principles, competing loyalties and competing claims.

Chapters 5 and 6 will look in more detail at these questions.

Chapter summary

In this chapter we have looked at:

- Values at work
- What is a profession?
- Professionalism

- Professional ethics
- Codes of practice for social work
- Social work values
- Real world dilemmas
- Social work paradoxes

We have tried to put the concepts of values and ethics into the context of social work as a profession. We have looked at what we mean by 'profession' and 'professional' and compared social work to other professions. We have at codes of ethics and conduct for social work and at the underlying values they imply, and we have considered the complexities of ethical decisions in the complex and even contradictory context of social work.

   In the next chapter we will consider one set of 'real world dilemmas' in particular: the ethical issues that are raised by the fact that social workers have limited resources at their disposal.

5 Ethics and Resources

- Competing claims on resources
- Principled rationing
- Assessments: advocacy versus fairness
- The duty of realism
- The duty to avoid waste
- Clarity about responsibility

One of the realities of doing the job of a social worker in practice is that resources are limited. There is only so much money in the budget, there are so many hours in the day. If we are to have ethical principles that work then they need to deal with the following inescapable realities:

- Social workers cannot always do the things that ideally they would like to be able to do – and have to make realistic plans based on what is actually available.
- Social workers are involved in decision-making about the allocation of resources. One of the main purposes of many social work assessments is to assist with decision-making about resources and social workers are regularly involved in decisions where there are competing claims on limited resources. (That is: where they have identified a number of different needs, but are not in a position to meet all of them.)
- Social workers are frequently involved in a process whereby they are, in a way, competing with other social workers for limited resources; and often the way that they present the case of a service user in a report will determine whether or not that service user gets access to resources.

It is our experience that many of the most difficult ethical dilemmas in social work arise from the constraints placed upon us by resources and for that reason we have decided to include a separate chapter looking more closely at this area.

Competing claims on resources

Social work services, in both the state and the voluntary sector, are limited in what they can provide by the resources available to them. However much they might like to expand to meet new demands and to address new areas of unmet need, they cannot do so unless either (a) additional resources are made available or (b) existing services are withdrawn or cut back. In this they resemble other public services which are delivered free at the point of delivery such as the police, the state school system and (in the UK) the National Health Service, but differ from private companies which can sell their services at a profit. For a private company, additional demand means additional income and this, in principle at any rate, provides the wherewithal for the company to expand to meet that demand. (Some private companies selling, for instance, residential care or fostering services to the state sector have been able to do just that.) But a public service with a fixed budget can spread itself more widely only at the cost of spreading itself more thinly. This fundamental difference between public and private provision is often forgotten when public services are encouraged to be more like 'businesses' and to treat their service users more like 'customers'. The reality of limited budgets means that social work practitioners in state and voluntary agencies are faced with certain characteristic dilemmas which can be summed up in the following two questions:

1   If we are asked to do task A and task B but only have enough resources to do one of them properly, should we concentrate on just one task, or should we try and do both even though we won't be able to do either one well?
2   If we decide to concentrate on just one of the tasks, then which one should have priority?

Decisions of this kind are being made every day in social work offices and we have already included several examples in exercises in previous chapters. For example, in Exercise 2.1 at the beginning of Chapter 2, we described an imaginary team of social workers discussing whether to try to continue running both a call-in surgery and a child protection investigation service, or to concentrate just on the latter. This was a general decision to be made about services being offered by the team, but essentially the same kind of dilemma arises when thinking about individual workloads, as the following exercise demonstrates.

Exercise 5.1

You are a childcare social worker in the statutory sector. Your special interest is working with children in the public care system who require placement in substitute families, but who are recognised as being 'hard to place'. You are working intensively with several such children, helping to prepare them for placement and to prepare foster families for their difficult task. It is generally accepted that to do this work successfully requires skill and a good deal of time. Up to now your caseload has been protected in recognition of this fact, and in recognition of the fact that inadequate preparation will result in an increased likelihood of placement breakdown (which would be difficult for the agency and, of course, disastrous for the children). You have had a caseload of eight such children at any one time.

However, staff shortages in the agency and an influx of child protection referrals have created a problem. Your manager says he has no choice but to ask you to take on some of these new child protection cases, over and above your existing caseload. This will involve you in joint investigations, attendance at child protection conferences and possibly court work.

How do you respond?

Comments on Exercise 5.1

We don't think there is an easy answer to this. The work you are already doing is difficult and time-consuming and very important, but so is the work that the manager is seeking to allocate. What is clear is that there is no possibility that you could take on this new work and carry on delivering the same service to the children on your existing caseload.

Your agency has a responsibility to protect children who seem to be at risk. But it also holds a parental responsibility for children in public care. Our suggestion is that, when social workers are placed in a position where they know they are unable to discharge their agency's legal responsibilities to vulnerable people (in this case children), they should ensure that steps are taken to inform those with overall responsibility for the service – including elected politicians – about the shortfall, making absolutely clear that, if task B is to be taken on, task A will not be properly carried out. We will return to this later under the heading of 'Clarity about responsibility'.

Principled rationing

In social work agencies, as in many other areas of public services, there is typically a division of responsibility in which front-line social workers assess needs but managers make decisions about how resources should be allocated. As one of us has observed elsewhere, this arrangement has some advantages for all concerned. Front-line practitioners can blame their managers for not making resources available to service users ('They don't care, all they think about is money!'). Managers in turn can dissociate themselves from the day to day contact with human distress and can blame practitioners for any casework that goes wrong (Walker and Beckett, 2003: 70).

We should not assume that this split of responsibilities is necessarily the most healthy way of running a social work agency (McCaffrey, 1998, suggests that it is an instance of the defence mechanism known in the psychodynamic literature as 'splitting'). And we should certainly be under no illusions, whether we are managers or practitioners, that leaving it to others to make difficult decisions somehow entitles us to take the moral high ground. A social worker who collects information that a manager will use to make decisions about priorities is morally implicated in those decisions. Likewise a manager who gives a social worker a piece of work to do, and inadequate resources to do it with, must share responsibility for the success or failure of that piece of work. (The inquiry into the death of Victoria Climbié rightly criticised senior managers for attempting to distance themselves from responsibility for the tragedy by saying that they were not responsible for the 'day-to-day realities' (Laming, 2003: 5)).

Psychological splitting does have the benefit to both front-line staff and managers of reducing anxiety – sharing out the pain – but too rigid a split between 'practice' decisions and 'resource' decisions ignores the fact that the two types of decision are closely intertwined. In reality, at *every* level of a social work agency, from practitioner to director, staff have to think not only about what it would be desirable to do in an ideal world, but also about what it is possible to do in the world as it actually is. And this involves making choices about who gets a service at any given moment and who does not. Even just in deciding how to divide up her time, a social worker is involved in making this type of decision, as the following exercise illustrates.

Exercise 5.2

You are working with the Green family on a variety of problems. You are aware that their problems are exacerbated by a lack of money. In particular, the family could really do with a washing machine (one of the children wets the bed) but cannot afford one. The benefits system

Exercise 5.2   (Continued)

(for whatever reason) cannot help. Your own agency is also unable to provide the necessary funds. Your manager says that this simply cannot be regarded as a high enough priority for a payment to be made out of the agency's small budget for one-off grants. However, a colleague tells you that you should be able to raise enough money by applying to charities. Your colleague tells you that the trick is not to ask any one charity for too large a grant but to make multiple applications to different charities asking for small contributions.

This looks like a time-consuming task. It will mean seeking out appropriate charities, finding out the application process in each case (which will often involve writing or telephoning to obtain application forms) and completing a series of applications, each in a slightly different format.

Many of the other families you work with also have financial problems, but you could not possibly commit this amount of time to obtaining funds from charities for each of them.

The time taken on applying to charities for the Greens will also be time taken from other work. For instance, you are behind on your visits to children in foster homes.

How will you decide whether or not you can justify spending time on applying to charities to pay for a washing machine for the Greens?

Comments on Exercise 5.2

You may well feel that we have asked an impossible question here. You would need to know more about the other cases and the other demands on your time in order to be able to decide how high a priority to give to the Greens and their washing machine.

On the one hand, you may have concluded that to make a decision about this you need to decide how serious the consequences would be for the Green family of continuing to struggle on without a washing machine, and compare this with the possible consequences of putting off or not doing the other things that you might have done with the time. This would be a utilitarian approach. (Refer back to Chapter 2 if you need to remind yourself of the difference between utilitarian and deontological approaches.) Given that you don't necessarily know the consequences of different courses of action, it would be hard to apply consistently.

On the other hand, you may have concluded that, if the Greens are eligible for financial help from a charity, then it is your duty to ensure that they get it, regardless of the time it takes you. This would be a more deontological stance. (Again: see Chapter 2 if you are not clear what this means. The difficulty with it is, of course, that there are only so many hours in your week.)

The main point we wish to make with this exercise, though, is simply that even an individual social worker, considering how to deal with her own caseload, is involved in decision-making about the deployment of resources which is no different in principle from the kinds of decision about resources that are made by senior managers or politicians.

What are the ethical principles involved in deciding how time and other resources are allocated? To date, most of the discussion of these kinds of question seems to relate to health services rather than to social work or social care. In the health field there is a substantial literature addressing such questions as the use of numerical 'quality of life' measures to determine priorities (Ovretveit, 1998) or the admissibility of taking the personal characteristics of patients into account when deciding how to allocate resources (Olsen et al., 2003) or the philosophical ideas underpinning resource allocation. Thus Girling (1993) suggested that, in a medical context, 'clinicians' ('practitioners' in social work terms) and their managers typically start from different philosophical bases when approaching these kinds of decision. Managers tend to adopt a utilitarian stance, Girling suggests, while clinicians are more comfortable with a deontological approach, which 'may incidentally account for the apparent fact that managers and clinicians sometimes seem to inhabit different ethical universes' (Girling, 1993: 41–42).

This observation about the philosophical gulf between managers and practitioners is relevant to social work agencies as well as to health services (even though in British social work, unlike in health care, most managers are themselves qualified practitioners). A social work manager who turns down a request from a social worker for funding on the grounds that others cases have higher priority may feel she is sincerely doing her best, in true utilitarian style, to deploy limited resources to the maximum possible effect. But the social worker may see the decision as a failure to recognise her service user's right to a better life and the agency's duty to provide it.

We do not propose to try to set down here which is the 'right' philosophical approach to such decisions. We discussed in Chapter 2 the merits and shortcomings of both deontological and utilitarian approaches. But you may like to consider for yourself how you would deal with the situation described in the following exercise.

Exercise 5.3

You are a social worker in a team whose task is to assess the care needs of elderly people. If you conclude that residential care is needed, the way that your particular agency operates is that you have to present the case for your client at a weekly panel, chaired by a senior manager. Funds for residential beds are limited, and the job of the panel is to decide who needs it most.

One week you have two cases to present to the panel, both involving elderly men who feel they need residential care. It happens that, in this particular week, no other cases are being presented, but the panel can only fund one residential bed.

You present the case as fairly as possible, for each of your clients (some details are given below), but the panel admits that it finds it difficult to decide between the two. After some discussion the chair of the panel asks you for your help.

'Both of these cases seem equally high priority to us,' the chair says. 'But you know these two men. Which of the two does your gut instinct tell you we should help first?'

How do you respond?

Mr Brown

Aged 84. Lives alone and has little in the way of extended family support. He is physically frail and has had a number of nasty falls requiring hospital treatment. He already receives a high level of homecare support, but it is not 24 hour and Mr Brown lives in fear of falling and hurting himself and not being able to get help.

Mr Rees

Aged 84. Mr Rees lives with his wife, aged 79, who is his main carer. He is physically frail and has had a number of nasty falls. Mr Rees and his wife have a very unhappy relationship. She resents having to care for him and there are some indications that the stress of it is taking a toll on her own health. Although you cannot prove it, you have a strong suspicion that Mrs Rees may be taking out her frustrations on Mr Rees himself. He seems frightened in her presence – even sometimes flinches when she comes near him – and, though he makes no complaints about her, is very anxious to move to residential care.

Comments on Exercise 5.3

One way of responding would be to say something like this:

'I'm sorry but I don't think that it is up to me to choose between the two. I think both these men need residential care, I have promised both of them I will do my best to obtain it for them and I have presented their cases as fairly as I can. I feel that I should leave the decision to the panel as to which of these men will lose out.'

In some circumstances such a position might be the best one to take. However in practice the choice will still be made and, if you are not prepared to participate in it, the panel – who do not know anything about either Mr Brown or Mr Rees other than what you have included in your report – will make it on their own. Perhaps, if you do have any sense that one of these cases should be a higher priority than the other, you ought to share your views with the panel?

If so, you would need to find some way of weighing up, for instance, the greater risk to Mr Brown of falling and lying undiscovered for some time as against the possibly greater risk to Mr Rees of being physically abused. You might do this by thinking in terms of absolute rights ('all elderly people are entitled to be protected against physical abuse' for instance) or you might adopt the approach of trying to compare the amount of suffering caused to each man in his present circumstances, or trying to compare the risks. The former approach is more 'deontological', the latter 'utilitarian', to refer once again to the philosophical positions we discussed in Chapter 2.

Assessments: advocacy versus fairness

Whether in a state-run agency or in the voluntary sector, social workers carry out assessments which look at the needs of service users and/or at risks they may be facing. The assessments may not be formal ones and they may not even be written down but they happen all the time. The information that social workers collect and the judgements and recommendations they make on the strength of that information are then used – either by the social worker herself or by others – to determine the type and intensity of service that will be offered, and indeed whether a service will be offered at all.

Given that any social work service has limited resources – a residential unit has only so many beds, a fieldwork team has only so many hours of social worker time, a daycare facility has a limit to the number of people it can take in – it is only ever possible to provide a service to one person at the cost of reducing the amount of services that are available to others. This, it seems to us, can place individual social workers in a difficult ethical position. Should she first and foremost be an advocate for her own client, presenting the client's case in as convincing a way as possible so as to maximise the chances of the client obtaining the desired service? Or, alternatively, should her primary obligation be to contribute to the agency's efforts to distribute its resources in as fair a way as possible, in which case the social worker might have to concede at times that her client's need was not as great as the need of others? (Exercise 5.3 highlighted this dilemma by posing a situation where a social worker was asked to choose *between* two of her clients.)

It seems to us that a social worker has a duty to do both these things – advocate for service users and contribute towards her agency being as fair (and non-discriminatory) as possible – but that these two duties pull in different directions.

To complicate matters still further, there is a danger that in advocating too rigorously on behalf of a particular service user, a social worker may actually do that individual service user a disservice by emphasising his level of need and/or the degree to which he is at risk, and thereby *labelling* him, in a way that may cause that service user problems in the future. An example of this would be if a social worker emphasised, or exaggerated, the level of risk to children in a family in order to get access for that family to resources which were only available to high-risk cases. This might be helpful to the family in the sense that it might indeed result in those resources being made available, but it could also result in the family being given a 'child protection' label which might colour their dealings with professional agencies for many years to come, particularly if (as proposed in the 2003 Green Paper, *Every Child Matters*) there are increasing moves towards centralised systems in which information is 'stored and accessed electronically by a range of agencies' (DfES, 2003: 53).

The duty of realism

One important ethical principle related to resources should be what might be called 'the duty of realism'.

In social work, as in other areas of life, there are many interventions which may be highly beneficial and desirable if undertaken properly, but which are better not attempted at all if they are not adequately resourced. A decision as to whether or not a given course of action is appropriate therefore often depends in part on whether or not the resources – money, time or expertise – are available to carry it out properly. This is very obvious if we think about contexts other than social work. Imagine, for instance, that the tiles on the roof of your house were getting old and the roof was beginning to leak. It might be desirable to replace them, but you would not consider removing them without first ensuring that you had the funds to pay for new ones.

In a social work context, though, we have sometimes heard it argued that, if a given course of action is desirable, it should be carried out *regardless of resource considerations*. This is the equivalent of removing the roof of a house without first ensuring that it will be possible to replace it, except that what is at stake in a social work decision is not just the fabric of a building but the well-being of a human being. To embark on a course of action without ensuring that it can be properly carried through is not just foolhardy, but irresponsible and unethical. It would be irresponsible, for instance, for a social work agency to remove a child from his family, without being reasonably confident that it will be able to meet the child's needs better than the family could. This principle is enshrined, in effect, in law in England and Wales under the 1989 Children Act which states:

> Where a court is considering whether or not to make one or more orders under this Act with respect to a child, it shall not make the order or any of the orders unless it considers that doing so would be better for the child than making no order at all. (Children Act, 1989, Section 1 (5))

Likewise it would be irresponsible for a social worker to embark on a programme of in-depth therapeutic work with a service user if she did not have the expertise or the time to carry it through properly, or if adequate support was not available for the service user in the event of him being distressed by the issues that came up in the course of the work.

On these lines, the British Association of Social Workers' Code of Ethics enjoins social workers to 'Recognise the limits of their competence and advise employers and service users when referral to a more appropriate professional is indicated' (BASW, 2002: 7). In the USA, the Code of Ethics of the National Association of Social Workers lays down the same principle in slightly different words:

> Social workers should provide services and represent themselves as competent only within the boundaries of their education, training, license, certification, consultation received, supervised experience, or other relevant professional experience. (NASW Code of Ethics, 1.04 (a): www.social-workers.org)

But ethical social work requires that we recognise not only limits to our own *competence* but also limits to what is *achievable*. As social workers we should not inflict interventions on service users which have a low chance of success or are likely to do more harm than good, in order to meet our own need to feel that we are 'doing something'. Nor should we pretend that the likely outcomes of our interventions are more positive than they really are in fact.

Exercise 5.4

When children cannot live in their own families, one of the tasks that social workers undertake is finding alternative families for them and preparing them for placement. It is generally agreed to be in children's interests to have the security of a single family with whom they can put down roots, whether this is an adoptive family or a 'permanent' foster family. In preparation work with children, such placements are sometimes described as 'forever families'.

However, research findings (see PIU, 2000) show that there is quite a high breakdown rate for such placements and that this breakdown rate increases with the child's age at the time of placement. About one fifth of adoptions of 7–8-year-olds break down, while for 11–12-year-olds there is a 40–50 per cent breakdown rate.

With such a high chance of breakdown, is it ethical for social workers to describe these placements to children as 'forever families'?

Comments on Exercise 5.4

This is a difficult question because how a placement is presented to a child may make a difference to the likelihood of success. (Too much dwelling on the possibility of breakdown may make a breakdown more likely.) However, for a child, to have a placement presented as 'forever' and then to have it break down can be an utterly devastating event. We cannot see that it is ethical to present a placement to a child as 'forever' when in fact the chances of breakdown are as high as 1 in 4 or even 1 in 2. It would surely be more helpful to the child to honestly admit the difficulties entailed in building a permanent bond between an older child and a family in which the child did not grow up, so that if a breakdown happens it will not come out of the blue and will feel less of a personal failure and a personal rejection.

The issue here, incidentally, is not just one of resources, because successful placement of older children cannot be guaranteed even with unlimited resources. But certainly limited resources are likely to reduce the chances of success.

The above exercise highlights the idea of 'permanency' in family social work. 'Permanency' (i.e. a secure home lasting throughout childhood) is indeed highly desirable for children and something that we should try to achieve. But, as June Thoburn cogently argues, we will not achieve the best possible outcomes for children unless we recognise that so-called 'permanent' placements do not necessarily in fact *provide* 'permanency'. Referring to a time when 'permanency' was very much a buzz-word in childcare social work, she writes:

> The reader of the statement 'the plan is permanence' at the end of a court report was led to believe that to plan for permanence was to achieve it. Little was said about the risks inherent in placement for adoption, which had to be balanced against the risks involved in children returning home or remaining in long term foster or residential care. (Thoburn, 2002: 514)

This is really a plea for realism in the sense that we have used the term. What Thoburn is saying is that, unless we are realistic about the risks inherent in adoption, then we will not accurately weigh up the benefits of adoption as a plan for a child as against the other available alternatives.

Realism

1. The attitude or practice of accepting a situation as it is and being prepared to deal with it accordingly …
2. The quality or fact of representing a person, thing or situation accurately or in a way that is true to life …

(*New Oxford Dictionary of English*, Revised Edition 2001)

Two points to note here:

- 'Accepting a situation as it is' should not be taken to mean that a realist should not challenge political or organisational constraints. Such things can and do change and therefore the possibility of change is in fact *part* of the 'situation as it is'. (Indeed it would be unrealistic to imagine that these things *don't* change!) But a realist, in her work with individual service users, should take into account what is likely to be available and achievable within the relevant timescale.
- The idea of 'realism' is not an uncontroversial one in academic social work where, in recent years, social constructionist ideas taken from other disciplines have been used to challenge the very idea of objective reality, and to suggest that all reality is created by human interactions. Parton and O'Byrne (2000: 22), for instance, state that reality 'emerges from the linguistic acts of persons'.

> ### (Continued)
>
> Social constructionist ideas are important. We have
> made use ourselves in this book of, for instance, the
> ideas of Foucault. However, we think there are plenty
> of realities which we can all agree on – that there is
> only so much one person can do in a single day, for
> example – and it is these rather basic kinds of reality
> that we have been referring to in this chapter.
>
> (We would also challenge the total relativism of
> some manifestations of social constructionism, but that
> is not a subject for this book. Readers interested in the
> philosophical alternative offered by 'critical realism'
> might like to look, for instance, at Houston, 2001.)

The duty to avoid waste

We suggested earlier that a 'splitting' of responsibility between managers
and practitioners for resource decisions on the one hand and casework decisions on the other may help both sides to reduce their anxieties, but cannot
ultimately absolve managers from responsibility for practice, or practitioners
from responsibility for resource management.

Given that the resources available to social work agencies are always
finite, it seems to us that front-line practitioners, as well as managers, have
a responsibility to ensure that the available resources are used to best effect.
Money and time should not be wasted on activities that are predictably
unproductive. Even when they are invested in activities that are likely to
bring *some* benefits, it is important to consider how these benefits compare
with the benefits that might flow from using resources in some other way.
(An expensive foreign holiday funded by a social work agency might benefit many service users but would the money spent on it achieve more if spent
in other ways?) Wasted resources are resources that could have been used in
other ways that would have brought more benefit to service users.

The following are some ways in which waste commonly occurs in social
work agencies:

- *Excessive information gathering*
  Elaborate, time-consuming assessment processes are wasteful when
  (a) the outcome is really a foregone conclusion, or (b) the recommendations flowing from them are unlikely to be carried out, or (c) the
  possible options are very limited and a decision could be made
  between these options on much more limited information. Indeed any

time spent on completing paperwork – or inputting information to computers – is wasteful if the information collected is not actually going to be used.

- *Inefficient use of information*

    In contrast, failure to gather or record information which *is* needed may result in enormous waste, if as a result (a) decisions are delayed, (b) inappropriate decisions are made, or (c) the same information has to be collected several times over. Even if the information *is* recorded, it may be wasted if there is an inadequate system for making use of it. Meetings, for instance, are wasteful if there is no mechanism whereby decisions made in the meeting can be translated into action. Beckett and McKeigue (2003), in a study on delay in care proceedings, found that time-consuming assessments sometimes seemed to repeat work already done by seeking for information that was already available on the record.

- *Ill-conceived interventions*

    Inadequately resourced interventions may achieve nothing, or may actually be harmful. Thus, far from *saving* resources, interventions which are not allocated a realistic amount of time or money, or are not carried out by appropriately trained staff, may end up being a waste of resources, and may necessitate more work in the future. For example, failure to provide an adequate response to parents struggling to manage the behaviour of their 5-year-old boy could mean that the agency may find itself having to accommodate him in residential care when he is 15.

- *Lack of clarity about aims*

    Interviews with service users can be a waste of time if the social worker is not adequately prepared and is not clear in her own mind what the purpose of the interview is. Large amounts of social work time can be used up, with no benefit to anyone, on pieces of work whose purpose is unclear either to the social worker or to the service user. If a social worker is visiting to provide 'support', for instance, she needs to be clear that the support is actually needed, or even wanted. (It can happen in such cases that a service user has no idea what the purpose of the social worker's visits are!) Similarly, if a social worker is visiting to 'monitor the situation', it is always worth checking whether these visits are yielding useful information that would not be available from other sources.

We should note in passing that waste of resources is far from being the only negative consequence of these instances of poor practice, even though it happens to be the one we are focusing on in this chapter. Apart from being wasteful, excessively elaborate assessments are an unnecessary intrusion into the lives of service users, and may unfairly raise expectations that cannot be fulfilled. Inefficient use of information and ill-conceived interventions are, at best, likewise an unnecessary intrusion, while at worst they can do actual harm to the service users they are supposed to help. (As we know from many child protection inquiries, inefficient use of information can even have fatal consequences.) And finally, apart from being wasteful, unnecessary and unwelcome visits are also a serious abuse of power.

Clarity about responsibility

Some readers, on the basis of what we have said so far in this chapter, may by now be wanting to raise an objection that would go something like this:

'You seem to be arguing that we should collude with the system in rationing out resources and cutting back services to people who need them. You seem to be arguing that we should simply accept the world as it is. Surely we should be challenging the system when it is inadequately resourced and fighting on behalf of service users to get the services to which they are entitled?'

We entirely agree that social workers should challenge the system. Indeed we would strongly argue that part of the 'duty of realism' is a duty on social workers to challenge inadequate provision by their agencies, rather than collude in the pretence that unrealistic objectives are actually attainable. Our point is that to attempt to take on impossible tasks is not the right way for either individuals or social work agencies to challenge the system. On the contrary, it serves to bolster up inadequate provision, by creating an unrealistic impression of what a service is really able to achieve.

Much of the public policy that social workers are required to implement – and much of the public criticism of social work that regularly takes place – does not fully pass what we might call the 'reality test'. Social workers are regularly asked to carry out tasks which are simply not possible with the resources available. One of us has argued elsewhere, for instance (Walker and Beckett, 2003: 68–9), that it was unreasonable of Lord Laming, in his report on the Victoria Climbié tragedy, to criticise social services departments for 'devising ways of limiting access to services, and adopting mechanisms to reduce service demand' (Laming, 2003: 11). Since they have limited resources and since their staff are not superhuman, social services departments quite obviously have *no choice* but to limit access to services and can only hope to do so as fairly and as transparently as possible. To suggest otherwise is at best muddle-headed and at worst dishonest. Was Lord Laming really suggesting that social services departments could meet all the demands made upon them, irrespective of their staffing levels and irrespective of the resources available to them?

The need to ration often results in social workers having to act in ways that go directly against the instincts which led them into social work in the first place – we are assuming that no one becomes a social worker in order to refuse a service to people who are in need – but it is no solution at all to pretend to be fulfilling duties which in practice it is impossible to meet. Far from 'challenging the system', attempting to do the impossible lets the system 'off the hook', creates a false impression that needs are being met when they are not, and allows blame to be pinned unjustly to individual social workers, or social work agencies, for the problems that inevitably arise. Part of the duty of realism is to publicly state when resources are inadequate to the task, being clear about the duties that are not being discharged and the risks that are being taken. This is clearly implied in the General Social Care Council's Code of Practice:

> ... 3. As a social care worker, you must promote the independence of service users while protecting them as far as possible from danger or harm.
>
> This includes:
>
> ... 3.4: Bringing to the attention of your employer or the appropriate authority resource or operational difficulties that might get in the way of the delivery of safe care. (GSCC, 2003)

Exercise 5.5

Lord Laming criticised social services departments for not routinely interviewing every child in need referred to them (Laming, 2003). Suppose you find yourself in a social work team where it is not actually possible to do this in the time available without dropping other tasks which are also important social work responsibilities. As the manager of the team, committed to realistic practice, what steps should you take?

Comments on Exercise 5.5

To interview separately every child in need referred to a social work agency is desirable. (The Climbié case tragically demonstrated that, even where the need presented by a carer is a purely practical one to do with housing or money, there may in fact be very serious child protection issues.) But whether it can actually be achieved in practice must depend (a) on the amount of social work time that is available and (b) on the competing claims being made on that time, which might include, for instance, carrying out child protection investigations, or visiting children in foster homes or residential care.

Our suggestion is that, if the team manager is not able to arrange for every child in need to be individually seen, then she should regularly place on record with the senior management of her agency (1) that she is not able to meet this expectation (2) why this is, and (3) what other competing claims on the time of her staff the team would not be able to meet if she insisted on every child in need being individually interviewed.

This would not just be a matter of the manager 'covering her back', or covering the backs of her team members, but also a matter of the manager fulfilling the ethical duty we have just discussed. If the team manager failed to let her agency know what was happening, then she would be being dishonest and would be depriving the agency of important information on which it might act.

To return to the analogy of the leaky roof that we gave earlier, what would our opinion be of a roofer who agreed to repair a roof for a given price and neglected to mention that, at this price, he would have to leave large holes in it?

Chapter summary

This chapter has looked at some of the ethical issues raised by the everyday reality of doing social work with limited resources. The topics covered have been:

- Competing claims on resources
- Principled rationing
- Assessments: advocacy versus fairness
- The duty of realism
- The duty to avoid waste
- Clarity about responsibility

The next chapter will look at the ethical questions raised by issues to do with power.

6   Ethics and Power

- Social work and the state
- Professional power
- Care and control
- Acknowledging oppression

In Chapter 2 we drew attention to the fact that ideas about values cannot be separated from the realities of power. We mentioned Foucault's observations about the close, two-way relationship between power and the ability to define what constitutes 'truth' in any given historical epoch, and we mentioned Marx's argument that the ruling class of a society will determine that society's system of values – 'rig' it, one might say – in its own interests.

Since social workers typically work with those with least power in society and yet are very often employed by the state – which is of course a major centre of power in society, if not *the* major centre – social work cannot afford to ignore the issue of power. The concept of *empowerment* and the idea of *anti-oppressive practice* (to which we will return in Part III) represent attempts to find ways of practising social work in which 'respect for persons' takes into account the huge differences in power that exist between one person and another.

Social workers themselves exercise a good deal of power, both formally, as a result of specific powers given to them under the law (for example, in the UK context, the 1989 Children Act or the 1983 Mental Health Act) and informally, as a result of their professional status and access to resources.

We are not going to go in depth into theories about power in this book. But in this chapter we explore some of the ways in which power is an issue in social work, and consider some of the ethical questions this raises. In summary those questions are:

- Social work's agenda is set for it, by and large, by the state and/or by powerful interest groups. How do we square that with a commitment to social justice?

- Like other professional groups, social workers have power arising from their professional status. How can we avoid this power being misused or abused?
- Social workers are often given considerable powers under the law to intervene in private life and enforce changes. When and how is it ethical to use these powers?
- Many of the people for whom social workers provide a service have problems which are directly related to structural injustices in society. How should we work with those individuals without seeming to treat their problems as if they are purely personal difficulties of their own?

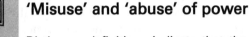

'Misuse' and 'abuse' of power

Dictionary definitions indicate that the words 'misuse' and 'abuse' have overlapping meanings. Both refer to improper use.

For us 'misuse of power' means power used inappropriately, while 'abuse of power' refers to the deliberate use of power by someone in a powerful position, for his or her benefit or gratification. However, this distinction is not always made and the words are often used interchangeably.

Social work and the state

The values espoused by social work's various professional bodies typically include the idea of championing social justice. In Chapter 4, for instance, we saw how the British Association of Social Workers identified 'social justice' as the second of five 'basic values' underlying the association's Code of Ethics (BASW, 2002). The National Association of Social Workers in the USA likewise places 'social justice' second in its list of 'core values' (NASW, Code of Ethics, revised 1999, available from www.socialworkers.org). The International Federation of Social Workers offers a definition of social work which puts social justice and social change at centre stage:

> The social work profession promotes *social change*, problem solving in human relationships and *the empowerment and liberation of people* to enhance well-being. Utilising theories of human behaviour and social systems, social work intervenes at the points where people interact with their environments. Principles of human rights and *social justice* are fundamental to social work. (IFSW, *Definition of Social Work*, 2000, available from www.ifsw.org; our italics)

Social work as a profession, then, seems to see itself not only as helping individuals but as bringing about structural change in society. And yet social work is an activity that is funded in large part by the state and has many of its functions and responsibilities determined for it by government. In Britain social workers in the statutory sector work within tight frameworks of government guidance which do not just set out their legal duties in general terms but provide detailed instructions on how to carry out those duties. (UK examples are, for instance, the *Care Programme Approach* in mental health, and the *Framework for the Assessment of Children in Need and their Families*: Department of Health, 1999, 2000). In England, even the regulatory body charged with maintaining professional standards (the General Social Care Council) is entirely government appointed.

How can a social worker be a servant of the state – the same state which is responsible for things like poor housing, unemployment, low benefits, low minimum wages and overcrowded schools – and still be on the side of social justice? How can a social worker implement the government's agenda and still consider herself as part of a force for social change?

There are, for course, no easy answers to these questions, but what does seem clear to us is that it is not enough to 'talk the talk'. Anyone can use words like 'anti-oppressive practice' or 'empowerment' or 'social justice'. But just to use the words is simply a form of tokenism. If they are to mean anything – and indeed if *any* set of values or ethical principles is to mean anything – it is necessary also to 'walk the walk'.

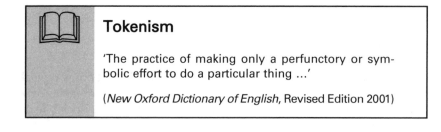

Tokenism

'The practice of making only a perfunctory or symbolic effort to do a particular thing ...'

(*New Oxford Dictionary of English*, Revised Edition 2001)

We suggest that a social worker who is committed to social justice – or even one who is simply committed to 'respect for persons' – needs to cultivate a degree of scepticism about the agendas she is expected to implement. The following exercise may help to illustrate what we mean by this.

Exercise 6.1

Suppose the government produces a new guidance document on the mental health services, which will have implications for social work in this area. The document states that its aims are:

Exercise 6.1   (Continued)

(a)   to improve the lives of people who have mental health problems,

(b)   to help the carers of people who have mental health problems,

(c)   to ensure that members of the public are adequately protected from the small minority of people who have mental health problems who are violent and may pose some risk to others.

What other, unstated, agendas, might also lie behind the document?

Comments on Exercise 6.1

Typically, a policy document of any kind will result from a process of negotiation between various interest groups, each with its own agenda. Agendas you may have thought of might include:

- the treasury agenda (pressure to save money);
- the agendas of various interest groups on whom the government relies for political support;
- the need of elected politicians to be seen to be 'doing something' about a particular event (for example an assault by a person with mental illness on a member of the public);
- the agendas of professional associations whose primary concern is the status and well-being of their own members;
- the commercial interests of particular industries (such as the pharmaceutical industry, or companies providing residential care).

A new policy, ostensibly intended to help mental health services users, will seldom, if ever, serve *only* that purpose and will almost inevitably include aspects which serve other purposes. These other purposes may or may not be consistent with the primary or ostensible aim of the policy.

This applies not only to the mental health services of course, but to policies in any other area. Child protection, for instance, is an area in which there is intense political interest and where policies will inevitably try to strike a balance between any number of different pressures and needs. We suggest that the following are all major factors in the development of the policies under which publicly funded social work operates:

'Something must be done'

If a tragic and well-publicised incident occurs – someone is assaulted by a person with a mental illness, a child is killed as a result of abuse which was not prevented by the child protection service – there is considerable public pressure on politicians for 'something to be done' to stop such incidents recurring. Politicians may be keen to demonstrate that yes, something is indeed being done, whether or not the 'something' will really help or is really justified by the facts. The 'something' may not necessarily be well thought through or implementable. It may even result in a *worse* service.

There are many situations in which a real improvement in the service would require a large additional injection of resources, but politicians are always facing demands *both* to improve services *and* to cut – or at any rate not increase – taxes. Arguably many new developments in social work and other public services represent attempts by politicians to be seen to be 'doing something' to improve services without actually increasing the resources being put into those services.

Cost-cutting

It is difficult for politicians to admit to cutting back services. Therefore cost-cutting exercises may be presented as innovative approaches. A good example of this is arguably the community care reforms of the 1990s, which were presented to practitioners and the public as an exciting new 'needs-led' approach, but were driven in large measure by 'the need to stop the haemorrhage in the social security budget, and to do so in a way that would minimise political outcry and not give additional resources to local authorities themselves' (Lewis and Glennerster, 1996).

Placating lobby groups

In developing new policies, politicians and civil servants will attempt to accommodate the wishes of lobbies and pressure groups that they perceive as being powerful. In the case of a new mental health policy, these lobby groups might include:

- organisations representing parents of people with mental illness;
- the professional associations representing psychiatrists;
- trade unions representing nurses;
- campaigning organisations representing the victims of offences committed by people with mental illness;
- civil liberties organisations;
- campaigning bodies representing people with mental illness;
- large charitable organisations which provide services for people with mental illness;

- the pharmaceutical industry;
- private companies – possibly organised into trade associations – which provide residential care and other services for people with mental illness. (The burgeoning new residential care industry was an important player, for instance, when the community care reforms of the 1990s were being thrashed out.)

Policy documents will typically include concessions which have been made to a number of different lobby groups. These concessions may be substantial or they may be little more than 'window-dressing' (what Cobb and Ross, 1997: 34, call 'symbolic placation').

The media

An emotive 'good story' often carries more weight in the media than a complex and difficult argument. Media coverage of dramatic incidents where mentally ill people have committed violent crimes may result in a public perception that these incidents are much more common than they really are and in pressure to 'do something' to stop them. This in turn may result in politicians and civil servants shaping policy around these concerns rather than around other, less newsworthy but perhaps more important, needs.

In the case of child protection, the media highlight both incidents where professional agencies fail to provide protection, such as the Victoria Climbié case (Laming, 2003) and incidents where they seem to have been overly intrusive, such as the Cleveland case in the 1980s (Butler-Sloss, 1987). These are relatively rare and extreme incidents and little media coverage is given to the day to day work of child protection agencies who deal with thousands of cases every day. Nevertheless, the high profile given to these cases means that they have a disproportionately powerful influence on the policy agenda.

Policy formation, then, is influenced by many forces other than a purely rational and altruistic consideration of the best interests of service users. This raises ethical questions for individual social workers. If the interests of service users were sacrificed in favour of other, competing interests (making politicians look good, keeping the social services department off the front page of the newspapers …) this would run counter to 'respect for persons' and would in fact be an instance, in Kantian terms (see Chapter 2), of treating people as 'means' rather than 'ends'. What should a conscientious social worker do if she feels she is being asked to implement policies which she does not feel are really in the interests of service users?

Ruby White, aged 91, is in hospital following a bad fall in her home in which she broke several bones in her right leg, necessitating surgery. Ruby was very badly shaken by the experience itself and also by the operation. She is anxious, tearful and slightly muddled as a result. She has lost all her confidence. She is very frightened by the prospect of returning home, even with the promise of a high level of domiciliary care, and would very much like a few days longer in hospital to recuperate a bit more, physically and emotionally, before she goes.

As the social worker for Mrs White, you can see that it is very much in her interest for her to be allowed this breathing space. You believe that a precipitate return home could have a serious impact on Mrs White's mental health and her capacity to cope in the long run. However, your agency is under tremendous pressure to move patients out of hospital wards where they are 'blocking beds' and indeed, under new regulations, your agency is charged a substantial sum of money by the hospital for every day that such patients stay on in hospital. Your manager instructs you to make arrangements for Ruby to return home tomorrow morning. He is simply not interested in discussions about the impact on Ruby's well-being. He says your responsibility is simply to arrange a package of domiciliary care to start tomorrow morning.

How do you respond?

Comments on Exercise 6.2

This case example revisits territory explored in the previous chapter. The reason for the pressure to move Ruby White is, of course, limited resources: the health service needs to vacate beds in order to have capacity for new patients needing to come in. It has to be acknowledged, therefore, that a decision to keep Ruby in hospital for longer might be in her own interests but might create more problems for some other elderly person – unknown to you – who needs to come into hospital. Your manager is not insisting you do this out of malice!

But there must be for all of us a point at which a system seems so inadequate that we no longer feel able in conscience to lend it legitimacy. We are not saying that this necessarily applies to the above case example. Many social workers are implementing just such a system and we are not suggesting that they are acting unethically in doing so (presumably they would argue that, given the resource constraints, a service like this is the best way of being fair to everyone). But a point may come for any conscientious social worker when she is asked to do something which simply seems wrong and which she is simply not prepared in conscience to do. Suppose, for instance that, in your judgement, the effect on Ruby of a premature return home could be fatal or irreversible: in such circumstances you might feel that your professional responsibility for her well-being was simply not compatible with going along with your manager's instructions.

You might try various means to get the decision reversed. For instance you might ask that the matter be referred to a more senior manager. You might advise Ruby and her family about ways in which they could appeal the decision. But ultimately, given that you are not actually in a position to act against your agency's own policies, you might be placed in a position where you either had to do something which you felt to be unethical, or to resign. Your decision would depend on how strongly you felt about the ethical principle at stake.

Politics in the voluntary sector

While the discussion has centred so far on state-funded organisations, it is worth noting that voluntary organisations are certainly not exempt from the kinds of competing political pressures that we have been discussing. Many voluntary social work agencies receive a good deal of their funding from the state, in which case they are as much an arm of public policy as statutory agencies. But even agencies with no state funding have their own sets of competing stakeholders to consider.

Hudson (1995: 37–8) points out that, while we might think that people work or become involved in the voluntary sector for entirely altruistic reasons, human motives are usually rather more complex than this. Hudson suggests that the following motivations also exist within voluntary sector organisations:

- People join governing boards of prestigious charities partly because of the recognition and status that comes with it, which may lead, for example, to more contacts with the powerful and famous.

(Continued)

(Continued)

- Donors may be seeking to improve their image or to gain influence over the organisation.
- Volunteers give their time partly as a result of a need for social activity and a friendship group, or perhaps as a stepping stone to a job or to improve their standing in the community.
- People may work in the voluntary sector because they are not comfortable with the kinds of pressures and/or constraints that exist in the public or private sectors.

It would be simplistic to assume, therefore, that political considerations are relevant only to state, or state-funded, organisations and that voluntary organisations are guided solely by the needs of service users.

Professional power

We have been discussing social work's relationship to power in society. We have suggested that an ethical social worker needs to consider the political context in which she operates and be aware of the possibility that there may be ethical problems with the policies that she is asked to implement, even if this is not immediately apparent, because these policies may serve the interests of powerful others as much as – or more than – those of the service users who are the ostensible beneficiaries.

But of course social workers exercise considerable power in their own right. The most extreme examples of this are the ways in which social workers are in some circumstances empowered to intervene in family life and restrict individual freedom, under childcare and mental health legislation. The ability of a social worker to exercise control over service users is not, however, limited to those situations where social workers are exercising (in their own right or on behalf of a court) powers given to them explicitly under the law.

For one thing, the fact that social workers are known to have these statutory powers is something that can give them considerable leverage *even when they are not actually using them*. For instance, the fact that social workers do, under some circumstances, remove children from the care of their parents, means that parents may feel obliged to fall in with the wishes of social workers even in situations where social workers have not been to court to obtain an order.

Social workers also have considerable powers arising simply from their position and from the relative vulnerability of their clients. For instance, working with people who have Alzheimer's disease or other forms of dementia may at times involve social workers making decisions to overrule service users' stated wishes in the interests of their own safety or well-being.

Social workers' control of access to services and resources can also give them considerable power. Service users may be expected to submit to a complex and intrusive assessment process administered by social workers in order to be considered for such services and resources, and the social worker's analysis of their needs may be crucial in determining whether or not they are successful in obtaining them.

Professions in general also have status and power in society arising from their possession of expert knowledge and skills or, to be more accurate, from the *belief* that they possess such knowledge and skills, whether or not they do in fact. Foucault argues that power is related to the ability to determine which kinds of knowledge count as 'truth' and which do not (see for instance Foucault, 1999) and certainly professions increase their power and status by making claims to special expertise.

Social work may not have the same professional prestige as medicine or the law but everything is relative and, in relation to many of their service users, there is no doubt that social workers often possess a great deal of privilege and power. Of course we hope that social workers use their power for the good of others but all power is open to abuse. Ethical social work practice requires us to be aware of the ways in which professional power can be, and is, abused. The following list draws heavily on ideas from Wilding's (1982) critique of professional power, though we have adapted them for our own purposes. It is important to note that not all abuses of power are malign in their intention. It is possible to abuse power with the best of intentions.

- *Excessive claims to expertise.* Professionals sometimes overstate their expertise. An example would be if you were to assert that, 'in your professional opinion' something was undoubtedly true, when in fact you did not have the evidence to make such a dogmatic assertion. There have been cases of miscarriages of justice arising from other professionals making excessive claims of expertise in the courtroom (At the time of writing, there is considerable interest in cases where parents have been convicted of murdering their children and/or had other children removed from their care, on medical evidence relating to 'cot death' that is now thought to be unreliable.) The abuse of power here consists of a professional getting his or her own view to prevail over the views of others on grounds which are in fact spurious. As Donald Schön noted:

  Whenever a professional claims to 'know' in the sense of the technical expert, he imposes his categories, theories, and techniques on the situation before him. He ignores, explains away, or controls those features of the situation, including the human beings within it, which do not fit his knowledge-in-practice. (Schön, 1991: 345)

- *Exaggerated claims of influence.* It can also be tempting to exaggerate your influence. For example social workers sometimes promise that they can provide a certain service when in fact the decision is ultimately not theirs to make, or mistakenly give reassurances which they are not in a position to guarantee.
- *Failure of responsibility.* This occurs where professionals have not properly carried out the duties entrusted to them. If, for instance, a social worker were to fail to carry out checks on a case as required under child protection procedures then this would be failure of responsibility and could of course result in a child being avoidably harmed.

  Sometimes it is impossible for resource reasons for a social worker to carry out all the duties that she has been given. *In these circumstances the social worker's duty is surely to make it clear to her employers that this is the case.* It would be failure of responsibility not to draw attention to the problem.
- *Abuse of position.* This arises where professionals use the power accruing to their professional status for purposes other than the best interests of service users. A fairly extreme example would be a psychotherapist who used the feeling of intimacy generated by therapy sessions to seduce a vulnerable client. But there are many other more subtle ways of abusing power which most of us have probably at some time been guilty of doing.
- *Disabling 'help'.* This is 'help' that has the effect of undermining the confidence of service users in their own capabilities and occurs when social workers do things for service users which they could actually do for themselves. What is particularly insidious about this sort of abuse of power is that the social worker and the service user may both see it as helpful (for instance, a service user may be grateful to a social worker who sorts things out for her, but may in the long run lose out if this means that she never learns to sort things out for herself).
- *Undermining personal responsibility.* This is really a specific kind of disabling 'help', which occurs when professionals undermine their client's sense of responsibility for their own actions. Think, for instance of the case of a habitual criminal offender, whom we will call 'Joe'. Professionals assessing his case and writing reports for courts have located the origins of Joe's problems in his difficult childhood. They may be correct but unfortunately they have presented this to Joe in a way which makes him feel that he has been absolved of responsibility for his own actions. ('Don't blame me for my offending. I can't help it. It's because of my unhappy childhood.') This may relieve Joe of some guilt, but it hardly helps him to take control of his own life. (We will come back to these kinds of issue in the next chapter when we look at 'Self-determination'.)

- *Neglecting rights.* Again, this may happen in situations where professionals sincerely believe that they are acting in the interests of service users. For instance, a service user's right to confidentiality, or right to be consulted, or even the service user's right to make mistakes may be bypassed by professionals who believe that they are doing so for the good of the service user.

The following exercise asks you to consider how social workers might misuse their power in each of these seven ways.

Exercise 6.3

Try and come up with one example, for each of the above categories, in which social workers might misuse their power. Try not to think of extreme examples, but of examples which might be encountered on an everyday basis. In particular we suggest that you try and think of examples that you could just about imagine being guilty of yourself.

Also ask yourself the following: In which circumstances is misuse of power of this kind most likely?

The seven headings are:

- Excessive claims to expertise
- Exaggerated claims of influence
- Failure of responsibility
- Abuse of position
- Disabling 'help'
- Undermining personal responsibility
- Neglecting rights

Comments on Exercise 6.3

The point we wish to make here is that misuse of power is not just some terrible thing that other people do, but something that any social worker is likely to fall into unless he or she is vigilant. This is why it is worth thinking about which kinds of misuse of power you yourself are most vulnerable to – and in what circumstances.

You may agree that the following circumstances make misuses of power more likely to occur:

- We may be tempted to make excessive claims to expertise at times when our own expertise feels under threat or when we are carried away by our subjective feelings. (For instance if you have a strong hunch that a child has been sexually abused, you may be tempted to say 'In my professional opinion there is no room for doubt that this child has been abused', even if in fact you do not have incontrovertible evidence and could be wrong.)
- We may make exaggerated claims to influence when we are anxious to placate a service user who is angry or distressed, or when we ourselves are secretly doubtful as to whether we have anything useful to offer.
- Failure of responsibility can result either from complacency or from being preoccupied with other things. It can result too from shortage of time or lack of support, though the responsibility of the social worker then becomes one of drawing attention to the problem and being honest about what can and cannot realistically be done.
- Social workers have abused their position in some appalling ways, as we can see from cases where workers in residential children's homes have physically and sexually abused children. But that is the extreme end of the spectrum. There are many ways of abusing your position which it is quite easy to fall into, such as using your professional status to impose your view of things over the view of a service user. For example, if you were defending yourself against a complaint by a service user you might use your status and your communication skills to win the argument. We suspect these sorts of petty abuse of power are more common than social workers might like to admit and arise particularly in situations where we feel insecure and vulnerable.
- We may be tempted to provide disabling 'help' sometimes because it seems quicker and easier. We may also be tempted to do it when we want to bask in the gratitude of the service user.
- Undermining personal responsibility is something that a social worker is very unlikely to set out deliberately to do, but can quite easily do inadvertently. It may result from a desire to be liked and to avoid confrontation. It is often easier to be 'understanding' than to be 'challenging', though good social work requires both.
- Neglecting rights may occur in a variety of circumstances. Sometimes the effort of consulting a service user (particularly if the service user is difficult in some way to deal with) may seem too much trouble. It may be tempting simply to bypass the service

user. Sometimes we may persuade ourselves that the 'end justifies the means' in a given situation. Social workers often rationalise being dishonest with service users (which really means neglecting their right to accurate information) on the ground that being completely honest would 'harm the working relationship'. This is often more about the social worker wishing to avoid discomfort, however, than about the service user's needs.

We argued earlier that the policies which social workers are required to implement are never developed with the sole purpose of improving the lives of service users: there are always other agendas involved. Likewise professional bodies, whose ostensible aim is to maintain professional standards and provide the best possible service, have their own agendas in that they tend to seek to enhance the power, status and working conditions of their members.

In our commentary on Exercise 6.3 we have tried to show that these multiple agendas are at play even at the individual level. Each of us as an individual human being, while trying to act 'professionally', also has our own personal agenda which will influence our actions and may, if we are not careful, lead us to misuse power. Honesty and self-awareness are therefore vital. It would be naïve and dangerous to assume that our own actions are necessarily beyond reproach, simply because of the job we do, yet some professionals do behave as if this really were the case. Writing from the perspective of the parents' group, PAIN, Sue Amphlett observes:

> During their training, childcare and protection workers are taught the child is their client and their only concern must be to act in the best interests of the child. Consequently the mantra for many of them is, 'We are working in the best interests of your child.' As a consequence many of them truly believe that they cannot be the cause of any harm to a child. (Amphlett, 2000: 175)

We have our own hidden agendas, sometimes hidden even from ourselves. Simply saying – or believing – that we only act in the best interests of service users does not mean that we necessarily do.

Care and control

Many texts speak of social work's dual roles of 'care' on the one hand and 'control' on the other, as if they were different, even opposite things. Thus the International Federation of Social Workers speaks of helping and controlling as being 'opposite aspects of social work' (IFSW, para 2.3.1 (2), www.ifsw.org) while Pamela Trevithick refers to 'conflicting responsibilities' (Trevithick, 2000: 140). But in fact in social work, as in other areas of life, care and control are not necessarily in conflict at all. We would not, for instance, consider a parent to be very caring if they did not exercise control over their toddlers' behaviour next to a busy road.

In situations where people are unable to take full responsibility for their own safety because of lack of understanding (as is the case with small children and roads) a professional duty of care may well extend to exercising some control over them. Similarly, in situations where people are at risk due to their own lack of power, professionals with a duty of care may need to exercise control over *others* in order to protect them. This applies to children who are being abused, where social workers may apply for court orders to intervene in, and overrule, families in order to protect children. And finally there are situations where control of service users is exercised in order to protect the public. This is one of the aims of the youth justice system, and is one of the reasons for detaining people compulsorily under mental health legislation.

'Control', used appropriately, is not the opposite of care, but on the contrary is an expression of care. We should not fall into the simplistic idea that the use of statutory powers is necessarily 'oppressive' or that working in other ways is necessarily anti-oppressive. (It would not have been an oppressive act, for instance, if the child protection agencies had intervened to remove Victoria Climbié from her great-aunt Marie-Therese Kouao (Laming, 2003).) Nevertheless, a number of dangers exist for social workers operating in contexts where the use of statutory powers is part of their brief:

- Frequent use of statutory powers may easily desensitise us to the seriousness of them.
- The fact that we can resort to these powers may tempt us to do so, even in situations which could in fact be resolved, given time, by negotiation and mutual agreement.
- The more that statutory powers are used, the greater the potential for social workers to become objects of fear in the communities where they work, thus eroding the trust that is required if they are to be able to work in supportive and non-threatening ways.
- Statutory powers can be abused to meet our own needs: to allay our own fears of losing control, for instance, or even to 'punish' a service user we have experienced as difficult.
- And yet, there is the opposite danger of failing to use statutory powers in situations where a vulnerable person is in need of protection.

As we have said before, self-knowledge is important in social work. The following exercise invites you to consider the ways in which you yourself might be likely to misuse statutory powers in your own practice.

Exercise 6.4

Imagine yourself in a social work job which includes, as a substantial component, the use of statutory powers (child protection, mental health, youth justice …). We have suggested above a number of ways in which bad practice can occur in that context. Given that we all stray into bad practice, in which of the ways listed above are you most likely to err?

In order to answer this question you may need to consider how you operate in other areas of life – and the feedback you get from other people.

For instance:

- Do people ever accuse you of being a 'control freak' or are you ever impatient with others?
- Are you aware of being someone who tries very hard to be liked?
- Do you enjoy the business of thrashing things out with people you have had differences with, or do you find this rather difficult and anxiety-provoking?
- Do you tend to avoid confrontation?
- Are you easily intimidated by angry or hostile people?

Comments on Exercise 6.4

Looking back over our own practice as social workers, we can think of instances where we erred both in the direction of failing to step in when it would have been better to do so and in the direction of seeking too quickly to take control and impose a solution. Either way, our own anxieties about losing control on the one hand, and about getting into conflicts on the other, will have played a part in our thinking.

Although taking control is not necessarily the opposite of 'care', the exercise of power is always open to abuse and those who are given power over others bear a heavy responsibility. The following are a few brief thoughts about how this responsibility should be exercised:

- *Clarity.* Resorting to powers which restrict the liberty of others is a serious decision to take and one that should only be taken for very clear reasons. It can be justified in terms of a legal duty of care towards someone who would otherwise be vulnerable.

- *Honesty and self-awareness.* These are important as there are many reasons why we might be tempted to reach for statutory powers when they really need not be used. There are also many reasons why we might be tempted *not* to use these powers even when they really do need to be used to protect someone. Unless we are honest we cannot separate out our legitimate motives from the ones that are really not legitimate.

- *Avoiding discrimination.* We need to be alert to the possibility that we may be inappropriately influenced – one way or another – in our decisions about the use of statutory powers by factors such as the ethnicity of the service user. Thompson (2001) notes that professionals are more ready to use 'control' in relation to black people than they are in relation to white people. On the other hand the Climbié report (Laming, 2003) discussed the possibility that the professional *failure* to intervene may have been partly the result of fears of seeming racist, given that Victoria and her aunt were of African (Ivorian) origin.

- *Respect for service users.* It is particularly important to work at this in contexts where social workers are in conflict with service users and are intervening against their wishes. There is quite a strong human instinct to distance oneself from people with whom one is in conflict and/or to respond in kind to hostility and anger. Good practice requires that this instinct is resisted.

Acknowledging oppression

In the board game Monopoly, players attempt to acquire property in order to accumulate rent from other players. It is, in a way, a simple representation of a capitalist society such as the UK. But, in one respect, Monopoly is very much fairer than real life: in the game all the players start off with an equal sum of money. Few people would bother to compete in a game of Monopoly in which another player was allowed to start out with ten times more money, for the outcome would be almost a foregone conclusion. But in life some start out with money, education, social connections, ability and personal confidence while others start out with none of these things – and yet no one really has the option of refusing to take part in the game.

There is one respect, though, in which Monopoly is rather tougher than the real world. In the game, the losers end up with nothing at all. In the real world, there is a safety net, albeit an imperfect one, in the form of a benefits system, social housing, free schools and hospitals and a variety of public services, one of which is of course social work.

But what function does social work play in the real life game of Monopoly? On an optimistic view, social work helps those who are losing out, equipping them to rejoin the game with a better chance of holding their own. But there is a more pessimistic way of looking at it. Perhaps social work is not *really* there for those who are losing out? Perhaps what social work really does is to serve the interests of those who are *winning* the game by making it look as if those who are losing are doing so because of their own individual failings, and not because of the unfairness of the game itself?

Social workers regularly encounter people whose problems are, in large measure, the result of circumstances outside their control. If they fail to cope with those problems, it is very easy to put labels on them which locate the problems inside themselves.

Exercise 6.5

Julie is a lone carer of three small children aged 9, 5 and 2. She has a lot to cope with. She has big financial worries and has several thousand pounds of rent arrears which were run up by her ex-partner, Hugh, who had an expensive drug habit. It was not unusual for Hugh to spend most of the family's weekly income on his habit.

Julie also has debts to pay off to fuel companies and several hundred pounds owing which she borrowed to pay for the children's Christmas presents.

Julie lives in fear of violence from Hugh, who resents the fact that she ended the relationship and comes to the house on a regular basis to make threats, ask for money or demand to be allowed to return. He beat her severely on a regular basis when he was living in the house. Getting him to leave was very difficult and took a great deal of courage. He still lives locally and boasts that he has friends in the neighbourhood who watch over Julie's every move. Julie herself has few contacts in the area. She grew up in care and has no contact with her own family.

Julie badly wants to move herself and the children to a new area, but there is no question of a housing transfer until she has managed to clear the rent arrears.

However, she is offered the opportunity of a cash-in-hand job, working nights, within fifteen minutes of her house. It would allow her to make some surplus money to pay off debts and work towards a housing move and the new start which she believes is in the interests of herself and the children. She has no one to leave the children with, but she teaches the older child how to contact her by phone, and takes the risk of going out at night to work, leaving the children alone in bed.

(Continued)

Exercise 6.5   (Continued)

Unfortunately for her, this is reported to Hugh by one of his friends and Hugh reports her to the authorities. When Julie admits to regularly leaving the children alone at night, there is a full child protection investigation, involving social services and the police, on grounds of neglect.

What are your thoughts on Julie's behaviour (assuming that all the above information is accurate and can be corroborated)? What should be the professional response?

Comments on Exercise 6.5

Obviously it is dangerous to leave such small children on their own, and the child protection agencies cannot just ignore this behaviour.

However, Julie's behaviour was not motivated by malice or lack of care for the children. It was a desperate attempt to remedy a desperate situation which was largely not of her own making. A woman with more money, or one who did not have the misfortune to have taken up with a partner who turned out to be violent and to have a drug habit, would never have needed to contemplate taking such a step. She would therefore never have had her competence to parent called into question.

A professional response which did no more than castigate Julie's behaviour would, it seems to us, be oppressive and an abuse of power. An appropriate response would have to acknowledge the difficulties that Julie was facing (how well would the rest of us do, if placed in her shoes?) and try in some way to support her in resolving her debt, her constant fear of violence and her conviction that a move to another area would give her and the children the new start that they need.

It is possible to argue that the only *real* way of resolving the kinds of problem faced by Julie in the above exercise is structural change at the political level. In a society where poverty is tolerated and men can get away with using violence to intimidate women, one might argue that problems such as Julie's will be bound to occur. We suggest that it is unrealistic to ask social work on its own to solve structural problems like this, but social workers do have a responsibility not to collude in 'blaming the victim'. As Neil Thompson puts it:

> There is no middle ground: intervention either adds to oppression (or at least condones it) or goes some small way towards easing or breaking that oppression. (1992: 169)

This is a topic to which we will return in Chapter 8.

Chapter summary

This chapter has looked at ethical issues related to power. The topic has been covered under the following headings:

- Social work and the state
- Professional power
- Care and control
- Acknowledging oppression

In Part III of the book we consider some key social work values and consider the issues involved in applying them in practice. We look first at 'self-determination'.

PART III

Values in Practice

7 Self-determination

- Self-determination and its limits
- Freedom and culture
- Responsibility
- Self-determination and social work
- Self-determination in practice
- Conflicting interests
- Paternalism and social control

Self-determination

'*Self-determination* is the ethical principle that persons should be permitted, enabled and encouraged to make their own informed decisions about the course of their lives.'

(*Blackwell Encyclopaedia of Social Work*, ed. Davies, 2000: 309)

In this third and final part of the book, we look at three broad areas in which complex value questions arise in day to day social work practice. In Chapter 8 we look at oppression – and what it might mean to practise 'anti-oppressively'. In Chapter 9 we discuss difference and diversity – and the issues involved in practising in an anti-discriminatory way. In this chapter we look at the concept of self-determination: the idea that social work has an ethical obligation to promote the right of service users to make their own choices in life.

Self-determination and its limits

The principle that social workers should respect and promote self-determination is generally agreed to be a cornerstone of good practice, but interestingly it is always presented with careful caveats. Thus the Code of Ethics of the British Association of Social Workers defines its first 'basic value' – 'Human dignity and worth' – as follows:

> Every human being has intrinsic value. All persons have a right to well-being, to self-fulfilment and *to as much control over their own lives as is consistent with the rights of others.* (BASW, 2002: 2, our italics)

and goes on to list, among other duties, a duty on social workers to

> ensure the protection of service users, *which may include setting appropriate limits and exercising authority,* with the objective of safeguarding them and others. (2002: 3, our italics)

In a similar vein, the National Association of Social Workers in the USA states the following, under the heading of 'Dignity and Worth of the Person':

> Social workers treat each person in a caring and respectful fashion, mindful of individual differences and cultural and ethnic diversity. Social workers promote clients' *socially responsible* self-determination. Social workers seek to enhance clients' capacity and opportunity to change and to address their own needs. Social workers are cognizant of their dual responsibility to clients and to the broader society. *They seek to resolve conflicts between clients' interests and the broader society's interests in a socially responsible manner ...* (NASW: www.socialworkers.org, our italics)

It would appear that a service user's right of self-determination should be respected, but only as long as it doesn't harm others, conflict with the interests of society, or harm service users themselves. The service user's right of self-determination is therefore provisional, and a social worker is very often placed in the position of deciding whether or not the service user's wishes are permissible. 'Of course even the most enthusiatic advocates of self-determination admit that there may be cases where the social worker has to take the decision out of the client's hands,' wrote Leighton et al. (1982: 13), 'but there is difficulty in saying precisely what the limits of self-determination are.' This makes the concept of self-determination hard to pin down and easy to set aside in practice.

Where the limits of self-determination should lie is a dilemma not just for social workers, but for society generally, with (as we'll discuss shortly) different cultures sometimes drawing the line in very different places. But the question is often brought into sharp relief in social work, for while promoting self-determination is generally agreed to be a key social work value, social work is also a profession which, to a quite unusual degree, is expected to exercise control over the lives of the users of its services.

In the UK, as we discussed in Chapter 6, social workers are given legal powers and duties to restrict liberty or to impose solutions on families and on individuals' powers under the 1983 Mental Health Act and the 1989 Children Act respectively. Social workers in residential settings working with young people, or with adults with learning disabilities, are involved in making decisions on what is permissible and what is not. Workers with young offenders are involved in monitoring compliance with court orders, and in taking young people back to court if necessary if they fail to comply. Social workers with the elderly, too, are involved in decisions where the wishes of service users are balanced against concerns about their safety and the wishes and feelings of carers and the wider community. In an analysis of decision-making in the case of a real life elderly service user – 'Mrs M' – Michael Horne concludes that:

> Mrs M's right to self-determination decreases as the concern and demands for 'something to be done' about her increase. The client's right to self-determination appears in this case to be principally a right that may be superseded by consideration of the interests and demands of 'society', which may be in conflict with those of the individual concerned. (Horne, 1999: 49)

'Something must be done', in short, seemed to trump user self-determination!

A cynic might say that what it boils down to is that a service user should be allowed to make her own decisions as long as a social worker agrees with them and as long as the social worker is not under pressure from others to do something different. This is perhaps *too* harsh. However, since there are circumstances recognised under which a service user's right to self-determination may be overridden, there is an ever-present danger that the perceptions, wishes and rights of service users will be buried and forgotten altogether under other agendas, when this is not really justified.

Freedom and culture

But why is self-determination important anyway? One answer to this question might be that it *isn't* necessarily, and that in fact the emphasis on self-determination – or individual freedom – that now exists in the industrialised countries of North America, Western Europe and Australasia is culturally specific. These countries were at one time commonly referred to as belonging to the 'Free World', after all, and while it is possible to debate how much freedom there really is in these countries, and how evenly freedom is distributed among their citizens, it *is* surely true to say that in these countries the idea of freedom (or liberty) is accorded very high esteem. Remember that 'Life, liberty and the pursuit of happiness' are the inalienable rights of man as defined in the American Declaration of Independence, that the motto of the French Republic is 'Liberty, Equality, Fraternity', or that Britain, in the famous patriotic song, is described as the 'Land of hope and glory, mother of the free'. In political discourse in contemporary Britain, 'choice', a synonym for freedom or self-determination, is another one of the things often assumed to be self-evidently desirable. That people should have more choice about where they go for medical treatment, or what schools they send their children to, is often taken as axiomatic. Whether people necessarily want more and more choice in these areas is a question that is seldom even raised.

But this isn't how things have always been seen and it isn't how they are seen in every culture today.

Liberal values versus social justice

Liberal values are also the values of capitalist society, a form of society which by its nature creates economic inequality. Freedom includes the freedom to get rich, and the freedom to fail. Arguably, in a liberal capitalist society, although everyone is notionally 'free,' only the better off are really free in practice.

Bill Jordan (1991) has even suggested that those social work values which are based on the traditional liberal values – such as individual self-determination – may actually be at odds with social work's social justice values (such as the commitment to 'The fair and equitable distribution of resources to meet basic human needs' (BASW, 2002: 3)).

Different cultures do not always place the same value on the autonomy of the individual as it is given in the West and may draw the line in different places between the rights of the individual and the rights of the community or group. Writing about the applicability of the idea of self-determination to Africa, and specifically to Zambia, Geoffrey Silavwe comments:

> When 'man' or 'woman' is defined only as a member of a group then 'self' is defined as within the group as well. In such a situation ... the closest one could get to the practice of self-determination is group self-determination. (Silavwe, 1995: 72)

He goes on:

> The principle of self-determination assumes a human need to make one's own choices and decisions concerning one's own life. The principle reflects

> social workers' recognition that people have a right to and a need for freedom in making such choices and decisions. It can only apply to social casework practice in a democratic society like Britain or the USA ... It is inappropriate in Zambia and Africa as a whole because the African pattern of behaviour is based on group determination. (1995: 73)

We need to be aware therefore that the exceptionally high value given to individual self-determination in the West is not necessarily given to it by people with roots in other parts of the globe, where, for instance, community solidarity or family cohesion may be seen as more important. We would not wish to overstate this. Even in countries like Britain or the USA, as we've seen, the right to self-determination is not absolute and can be 'trumped' (as we have put it) by many other considerations, so the differences between cultures are differences of degree. But serious misunderstandings can result from assuming that people of every culture view these matters in the same way.

Responsibility

Whatever the differences between cultures in the extent to which *giving* choice to individuals is desirable, it is surely the case that every culture expects individuals to be responsible for their choices in a moral sense. The concept of individuals being answerable for their own choices between good and evil is not only a part of conventional Christian belief but, as we discussed in Chapter 3, of conventional Islamic belief also:

> Each man shall reap the fruits of his own deeds: no man shall bear another's burden. (The Star 53: 38 in *The Koran*, trans. Dawood, 1990)

Even in a culture in which group determination might be considered more important than self-determination, individuals are held to account for their own actions. Silavwe (1995: 75) writes that, in traditional Zambian culture: 'where a man is a habitual wrong doer, the whole village community may assemble at a beer party and openly curse him'.

Immanuel Kant believed that, although we cannot prove that our actions are not predetermined in some way (and many modern psychologists and biologists might argue that they are) nevertheless we can't help but think of ourselves as making free choices if we are to act at all. A moment's reflection will confirm that he was right. Even if you take the view that your personality is entirely the product of 'nature and nurture', you have no alternative but to think of yourself as a free agent in the moment when you are deciding what to do next. 'Nature and nurture' may help to explain why you make the decisions you make, but they will not make the decisions for you.

The idea of the will as 'autonomous' was, for Kant, the 'supreme principle of morality' (Walker, 1998: 39). At the beginning of this book we took the same position when we stated that values and ethics are concerned with the basis on which we make choices. (In fact, if we did not believe that we had choices, there would be no point to this book.) The notion of individual choice is pretty fundamental to what makes us human. If this is so, then to deny or restrict someone's belief in their own capacity for self-determination would be to deny their humanity: which is the very essence of oppression, as we will discuss in the next chapter.

But it is worth noting that there are different ways of looking at what it means to promote self-determination. Does it mean maximising choices for people, or does it mean allowing people to take responsibility for their own actions?

Exercise 7.1

You are writing a report for a criminal court on a young man called Ben, who is accused of a series of offences of theft. If Ben is found guilty, your report will be used by the judge when deciding what sentence to pass. You are aware that this young man has had a very unhappy childhood. From an early age, it seems, he has been abused, rejected, ignored. Throughout his life Ben's parents have always had other priorities than Ben himself. It seems to you that he has every reason to feel angry with the world.

Ben asks to see the report you have written about him. When he sees it his first comment is this:

'So you're saying I couldn't help myself, right? You're saying it's not my fault that I steal stuff. It's because of my mum and dad.'

How do you respond to this in a way that promotes Ben's self-determination?

Comments on Exercise 7.1

Social workers tend to look for explanations for things and – rightly – try to avoid making moral judgements about those they work with. Explanations are useful in a situation like this. Clearly it would be simplistic and unjust simply to characterise Ben's problems as being no one's fault but his own.

But Ben's question highlights a difficulty. In offering explanations for things, we are in danger of undermining people's sense of being in charge of their own lives. Although Ben might be glad to be offered someone else to blame for his problems, in the long run it is not going to be terribly helpful to him to see all the fault as lying with other people.

So some care is needed when considering how to answer Ben's question. Perhaps something on these lines:

'No. You could help yourself. You could have decided not to steal. I'm just pointing out to the judge that you may need a bit of help to see that.'

Self-determination and social work

Why should self-determination be an important principle in social work? Many would take the deontological position that self-determination is a *right* – and part of what it means to be human – and therefore something we have a basic moral *duty* to respect and promote.

But in a social work context, there is also a straightforwardly utilitarian argument for adopting a form of practice that promotes service users' belief in their ability to manage their own lives. Firstly it will enable the service user to cope with more of her own problems, which will very probably be a satisfactory outcome for her. Secondly it is a much more efficient use of resources than an approach which requires the service user to come to the social worker for help over a long period. This kind of thinking underlies Task Centred social work (Reid, 1978), which developed from the observation that long-term involvement was not necessarily any more effective than short interventions. Brief (or Solution-Focused) Therapy (de Shazer, 1985) is based on the similar idea that instead of trying to get to the bottom of problems, therapy should be aimed at promoting a service user's capacity for problem-solving.

Another reason why it is particularly important to think about questions of self-determination is that social work largely specialises in working with people who are in relatively powerless positions in society such as children, disabled people, elderly people and people with mental health problems. Poor people are also heavily over-represented in many social work caseloads, particularly in the children and families field. (Gibbons et al., 1995, for instance, found that in their sample of children who had been on child protection registers, 57 per cent came from families without a wage earner.)

And when we speak of these groups of people being relatively powerless, what we really mean is that they are relatively constrained in the extent to which they can determine their own lives. If you are poor, for instance, you have the capacity to exercise choice, but your opportunities for exercising it are of course limited by your lack of purchasing power. If you have a learning disability your options are likewise constrained not only because you are likely to be poor, but because of your disability. One could similarly catalogue constraints on choice faced by elderly people, people with physical disabilities and people with mental health problems.

So those with whom social workers deal are typically faced with restrictions on their ability to exercise choice. Additionally, powerlessness has a tendency to become a vicious circle, as Malcolm Payne describes:

> If people have important experiences which show that what they do does not affect what happens to them, they form the expectation that their actions will not produce any useful results. Their capacity to learn useful behaviour in other situations becomes impaired. (Payne, 1997: 283)

This is another reason why promoting self-determination is central to social work: it is a matter of seeking to redress or reduce difficulties created by structural injustices and supporting marginalised groups in taking back power for themselves. Promoting self-determination in these terms surely relates very well to social work's difficult but often stated commitment to promoting social justice (rather than being at odds with it, as Bill Jordan, 1991 suggested). Thinking of this kind lies behind the development of ideas like empowerment (Solomon, 1976) and User Advocacy (see for instance Brandon et al., 1995) as approaches in social work, and behind the idea of anti-oppressive practice (e.g. Dalrymple and Burke, 1995), which we will discuss in the next chapter.

Self-determination in practice

It is easy to say that it is important to promote self-determination. It is sometimes harder to see what this might mean in practice. Consider the situation outlined in the following exercise.

Exercise 7.2

A man goes to his doctor and tells her that he is suffering from depression and that he wishes her to prescribe anti-depressants for him. The doctor declines. She says that anti-depressants can have bad side-effects and can create dependency and be difficult to come off once you are on them. She also says that they are a costly resource, like most drugs, and therefore shouldn't be used until other options have been tried.

> ### Exercise 7.2   (Continued)
>
> She asks her patient whether his depression is the result of events in his life and whether perhaps he needs some counselling, or even just to take time to work through whatever has been happening for him.
>
> He says that he is not obliged to discuss his personal life with his doctor. He says that he has looked into the matter carefully himself, having been reading up about depression and its treatment in books and on the internet, and he feels he has reached an informed decision about what he needs. He feels that the doctor should respect his decision, rather than trying to impose her own views.
>
> Do you agree with the patient, or do you think the doctor is justified in her position? Where does the principle of 'user self-determination' (or in this case 'patient self-determination') fit in?

Comments on Exercise 7.2

We think the doctor is justified in her position. She has a responsibility not to prescribe medication to her patients if she thinks it may be bad for them. She also has a responsibility, as she says, not to waste the scarce resources of the NHS. Clearly she should listen to her patient, be respectful of his views and keep an open mind, but she is not obliged to give him what he wants.

(If you disagree with us in this instance, incidentally, we are sure you can think of other instances where you think it would be wrong for a doctor to prescribe drugs on demand.)

Arguably the doctor is denying her patient his right to self-determination since she is not letting him make his own choices about how to deal with what he believes is depression.

However, there is a case for saying that she is actually promoting self-determination. She is suggesting to the patient that, instead of seeing his depression as something external to himself to be 'fixed' by chemicals, it could be that if he examined his own life and took some responsibility for the way he now feels, he might be able to resolve things for himself.

You can doubtless think of further arguments on both sides, but what we would like to draw to your attention here is that respecting user self-determination has a deeper meaning than just 'doing what the user wants'. We suggest that the ethical obligation to respect user self-determination could usefully be described as the obligation *not to do things for or to our service users except when we believe this is likely to enhance their ability to manage their own lives.*

It follows from this that sometimes it is appropriate to go *against* the wishes of a service user in order, in the long run, to promote their ability to cope with their own lives. The scenario in Exercise 7.3 illustrates this.

Exercise 7.3

Roger is a social worker in a multidisciplinary team that provides support to adults with learning disabilities living in group homes. One of the group home residents, Angie, arrives in his office having got in a muddle with her benefits, with the result that she currently has no money and is in a very distressed state. She asks Roger to sort it out for her.

Roger gives her some sympathy, calms her down, makes her a cup of tea and then goes off and sorts the whole thing out on the phone with the benefits office. Angie is very grateful.

Roger has respected Angie's wishes and done exactly what she asked of him. Has he therefore supported her right to determine her own life?

Comments on Exercise 7.3

You will probably agree that, while Roger has done exactly what Angie wanted, he may not really have done her a good turn. What he has done is to encourage her to bring her problems to him to sort out: to be dependent on him. He might have done better to have talked Angie through what she needed to do, given her a phone and then given her the tea and some praise after she had sorted it out for herself. She might not have liked it at first, but he would have been encouraging her to develop her own problem-solving skills and therefore develop her capacity to manage her own life.

The trouble is that, just as Roger was encouraging Angie's dependent behaviour, so Angie was encouraging his helpful behaviour by being happy and grateful when he had sorted it out for her. Dependency can be rewarding in the short term for both social worker and service user – though it is ultimately disabling for both – and we would suggest that every social work office has service users, not necessarily learning disabled, who have got into a pattern of taking their problems in for the social workers to solve.

These service users are manifestly not people whose capacity to determine their own lives has been enhanced by the agency, even if the agency has done its best to act on their wishes.

The commitment to supporting self-determination could be viewed as being about *either* (a) following the service user's views and wishes, *or* (b) promoting the service user's capacity to determine her own life. This is the distinction between so-called 'negative freedom' and 'positive freedom' which is made by several writers on social work values (for example Horne, 1999: 13–23). The first is called 'negative' because it is about *not restricting* a person's choices (the right to free speech under Article 10 of the European Convention on Human Rights is an example of a negative freedom in this sense). The second is called 'positive' because it is about *promoting* a person's capacity to make choices.

As illustrated by the example of 'Angie', there are very good arguments for interpreting user self-determination in the second way. The danger of course is that the idea of positive freedom could be misused to justify coercion and restriction of choice with the argument that in the long run it will increase self-reliance.

Conflicting interests

The examples we have given so far have focused on the simplest situation where the relationship between professional and service user is one to one. New considerations enter the equation when there are other people involved, as the following exercise illustrates.

Exercise 7.4

As in Exercise 7.2, a man goes to see a doctor and asks for the doctor to accept a diagnosis he has made himself and to provide the treatment that he thinks is necessary.

But this time the man is the widowed father of a 5-year-old boy and it is the boy who is really the patient. He is behaving in a way which

(Continued)

Exercise 7.4   (Continued)

his father finds very difficult to manage. His father has done extensive research into the matter and has concluded that his son definitely has ADHD (Attention Deficit Hyperactivity Disorder). He wants the doctor to prescribe the drug Ritalin for his son.

The doctor asks if there might be another explanation for his son's behaviour. Perhaps the father would benefit from advice on managing the behaviour? Perhaps the boy is grieving for his mother?

The father becomes angry. He suggests that the doctor is accusing him of not being an adequate parent. He accuses the doctor of discriminating against him as a single father and says that if he had been a woman the doctor would not have questioned him like this. He repeats that he is sure that his son has ADHD. He says that as the boy's father he knows far more about his son than the doctor could ever hope to know, and that the doctor should therefore accept his diagnosis and act on it.

What should be the doctor's position here?

Can you think of situations analogous to this that arise in social work?

Comments on Exercise 7.4

Obviously the doctor should be sympathetic to the father's distress (single fathers do often feel that the world assumes them to be incompetent and perhaps he is still grieving as well as his son) and she should take his views seriously. However it is even clearer here than it was in Exercise 7.1 that the doctor cannot possibly just accept the father's view, because in this situation someone else's rights and needs are also at issue: the son's.

Ritalin does undoubtedly have side-effects and being given the 'label' of an ADHD diagnosis could have lifelong implications for the boy.

The doctor has a professional responsibility therefore not just to accept the father's view but to insist that a proper assessment is carried out of the child's behaviour problems and their causes before any treatment is offered.

In this scenario, although both father and son are the doctor's patients, the service user whose needs are primarily to be considered is the son: he is the one who has been identified as having a problem, and for whom treatment is being sought. Since the son is really too young to make an informed decision, this places a particular responsibility on the doctor to ensure that she considers what the son's interests are.

A couple of social work parallels:

1   The carer of an elderly person (or a person with a disability) insists that this person is placed in a residential home, for her own good, and says: 'She'll say she doesn't want to go but you will just have to persuade her, because it's clearly in her best interests.'
2   Child and family social workers are frequently in this sort of position, since they must work with parents, but their primary responsibility is towards children. Although they should respect the fact that parents know much more about their children than they do, and respect the fact that, in most cases, parents love their children and want what is best for them, they cannot (any more than the doctor in the exercise) simply accept the parents' viewpoint.

So, when we are dealing with a situation in which more than one person is involved, it would make no sense to interpret the principle of user self-determination as meaning that we should simply accept and act on the viewpoint of one of them even – in fact *especially* – if that individual is the only one capable of articulating a view.

Paternalism and social control

We will conclude this chapter by looking at two strands in social work practice which certainly conflict with user self-determination in the 'negative freedom' sense, and have the potential to conflict with user self-determination in the 'positive freedom' sense:

- In some circumstances social workers take away or restrict the right of service users to make choices for themselves, but do so in the belief that they are acting for the service user's own good. This we will call 'paternalism'.
- In some circumstances social workers take away or restrict the right of service users to make choices for themselves, but do so in the belief that they are acting for the good of *society in general*, or of people *other than the service user*. We will call this 'social control', using the phrase in a rather specific sense for the purposes of this chapter.

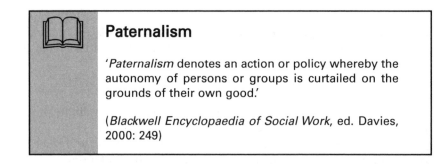

Paternalism

'*Paternalism* denotes an action or policy whereby the autonomy of persons or groups is curtailed on the grounds of their own good.'

(*Blackwell Encyclopaedia of Social Work*, ed. Davies, 2000: 249)

The word 'paternalism' comes, of course, from the word 'paternal', which in turn comes from the Latin word *pater*, or father. Used in the context of social work, it therefore implies a fatherly (or at any rate *parental*) relationship between social worker and service user. (In the UK the word *maternalism* might be a more appropriate term, given that British social workers are mainly women, but it is not a word in general use, for reasons which it would be interesting to discuss, but which are outside the scope of this chapter.)

Paternalism, then, implies a parental relationship. It is generally accepted that parents are required at times to restrict a child's 'negative freedom' in his longer-term interests. An obvious example would be a situation in which a small child wanted to jump into the deep end of a swimming pool, or into the path of an oncoming bus. In fact parents impose all kinds of restrictions on their children's freedom of choice, and no one really disputes that this is right, necessary and in the interests of a child. Family social workers often encounter children whose behaviour parents have, for whatever reason, failed to moderate and control. Such children are not happy, tend to have serious problems in socialising with other children, and may have other problems too such as being overweight or having bad teeth as a result of being able to eat whatever they want.

Parenting, then, is a good instance of a situation where it is appropriate to restrict negative freedom in the interests of promoting positive freedom in the long run. But is parenthood an appropriate model for professionals dealing with adults who may be as old as or older than themselves? And when does paternalism of this kind constitute a kind of oppression in the form of a denial of adult status? To make it more complicated, in many situations it is debatable which is really the most paternalistic course of action, as the following exercise illustrates.

Exercise 7.5

In Exercise 7.3, we described the case of Angie, a woman with a learning disability, who came to a social work office to ask her social worker

---
Exercise 7.5   (Continued)

Roger for help with a benefit problem. As far as we can see, unless he refused to get involved at all, Roger had two options:

- Contact the benefit office and sort the problem out himself on her behalf.
- Give Angie some support and encouragement in sorting it out herself.

The former is what Angie actually wanted and asked him to do.

The latter, we argued earlier, might in the long run be more in her interests as it would help her to develop her own ability and confidence in solving problems for herself.

Suppose that Roger was anxious to avoid behaving in a paternalistic way. Which course of action should he take?

Comments on Exercise 7.5

Our suggestion is that either course of action could be described as paternalistic.

By simply sorting the problem out for her, Roger would be treating Angie as if she was not an adult capable of sorting things out for herself (and giving Angie that message about herself).

On the other hand, if he declined to do what she asked, on the grounds that he considered that it would be in her best interests to sort it out for herself, then he would be paternalistically deciding that he knew better than she what was really in her best interests.

What this demonstrates is that, by its nature, social work is always to a certain degree paternalistic.

 **Social control**

Although the *Blackwell Encyclopaedia* gives no definition of 'social control', we will adapt the Encyclopaedia's definition of paternalism (quoted above) to

(Continued)

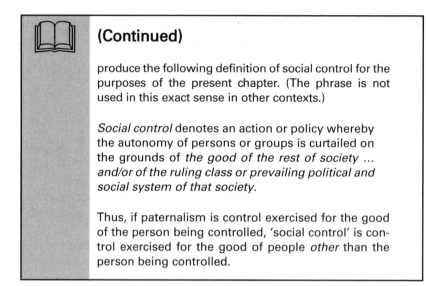

(Continued)

produce the following definition of social control for the purposes of the present chapter. (The phrase is not used in this exact sense in other contexts.)

Social control denotes an action or policy whereby the autonomy of persons or groups is curtailed on the grounds of *the good of the rest of society ... and/or of the ruling class or prevailing political and social system of that society.*

Thus, if paternalism is control exercised for the good of the person being controlled, 'social control' is control exercised for the good of people *other* than the person being controlled.

Most tasks which social workers perform for the good of the rest of society are arguably performed for the good of the individual concerned as well. For example social workers working with young offenders may be trying to reduce juvenile crime and therefore reduce the nuisance and distress caused by young offenders to the rest of the community, but they would probably also see themselves as trying to promote the interests of young offenders too by helping them to move on from crime to more constructive kinds of activity.

Similarly (in the UK) Approved Social Workers under the Mental Health Act 1983 can make applications to detain mentally ill service users under Sections, 2, 3 or 4 and 'with a view to protecting other persons', but would probably usually feel that a person who might harm others should be prevented from doing so in her own interests as well as in theirs.

Some social work, though, arguably has a more insidious social control function. As Neil Guterman points out, the poor are typically subjected to far 'greater scrutiny by public authorities' (2001: 27) than the rest of society. Middle- and upper-class neighbourhoods would be up in arms, we suspect, if schools, doctors, police and social services shared information about families in the way that happens routinely in poorer neighbourhoods. One could argue that such scrutiny, justified in the name of child protection, serves another unstated function: that of 'keeping the poor in their place'.

When social workers' actions have a social control component, the questions they need to ask themselves are:

- Is this action in the long-term interests of the service user?
- If not, is it protective of the legitimate interests of others in society to an extent that outweighs the intrusion on the liberty of the service user?

If the answer to both of these questions is no, it seems to us the action is professionally unethical.

Exercise 7.6

Try and think of some circumstances in which social workers and other professionals might be asked to act as agents of social control, but where this could not be ethically justified.

Comments on Exercise 7.6

You may have thought of some better examples, but the following are a couple of suggestions:

1 Pressure is brought to bear on social services by the local councillor, MP and vocal local residents, to 'remove' an elderly man whose eccentric lifestyle is said to be bringing a bad name to the neighbourhood and potentially affecting property values. The man concerned does not live in unsafe or unhygienic conditions, but he has decorated his garden in very lurid style and placed large noticeboards in very prominent positions stating his view that the end of the world is near, and he wears long flowing robes, has a long beard and goes about barefoot in all weathers.

   Social work agencies do sometimes come under pressure to 'deal with' people whose only offence is an unorthodox lifestyle which others find embarrassing or uncomfortable. It is surely unethical to deprive someone of their right to self-determination on such grounds.

2 In the former Soviet Union, certain people were detained in psychiatric institutions, not because they were mentally ill, but because the government did not like and felt threatened by their political views.

   Detaining these people was not in their own interests and nor did it protect society at large. It served only the interests of the then ruling elite. Even if the doctors involved were acting under instruction from their employers, and perhaps according to the requirements of their employment contracts, their behaviour was professionally unethical, as would have been the behaviour of any social worker involved in the same process.

Chapter summary

This chapter has explored what is meant by promoting self-determination. It has considered the difficulties in defining it in practice and the other calls made on social workers that may conflict, or seem to conflict, with promoting self-determination. We have suggested that, in spite of these difficulties, this is a crucial social work value, and have set out some reasons why this is so. The topics covered were:

- Self-determination and its limits
- Freedom and culture
- Responsibility
- Self-determination and social work
- Self-determination in practice
- Conflicting interests
- Paternalism and social control

The next chapter will consider the nature of oppression, and will look at respect as being in a way the antithesis of oppression.

8 Oppression and Respect

- What is oppression?
- Levels of oppression
- The internalisation of oppression
- Oppression, objectification and 'respect for persons'
- Oppression and discrimination
- Can social work counter oppression?
- Minimum intervention/maximum partnership

The term 'anti-oppressive practice' is repeated like a mantra in social work education, to the point that it is in danger of losing its meaning and becoming merely a comforting sound. But since social workers deal with people who experience oppression, and since social work is itself capable of being very oppressive in its own right, oppression is something that social workers really need to take very seriously. This involves somehow getting to a place in our minds where oppression is not simply something 'out there' but something we have some sense of from the inside. Some readers of this book will not find this hard, as many will have plenty of experience of oppression at first hand to draw upon. For others, it will require more imagination. (For instance, one of the authors of this book – Andrew – is able to draw on direct experience to understand the effects of racism; the other – Chris – has to work quite hard to begin to imagine what it would be like to like to be on the receiving end of racism.) But to be a social worker without some grasp of the nature and effects of oppression would be, in our opinion, like being a doctor without a grasp of the nature and effects of bacteria. 'Oppression' and 'anti-oppressive practice' may be in danger of becoming meaningless buzz-words, but the underlying concepts are crucial.

'Respect', the second subject of this chapter, is the other side of the coin. Oppression involves denying a person respect. Properly applied, it seems to us, the principle of 'respect for persons' must amount to roughly the same thing as 'anti-oppressive practice'.

Before going any further, you might like to take time out to consider your own definitions of (a) oppression and (b) respect.

Comments on Exercise 8.1

We can't guess what definitions you might have come up with. Our own thoughts about these questions are set out in the rest of this chapter.

What is oppression?

Oppression

Oppress: lie heavy on, weigh down, (spirits, imagination, etc.); govern tyrannically, keep under by coercion, subject to continual cruelty or injustice ...' (*Concise Oxford Dictionary*, 7th Edition, 1982)

Oppression: 'Inhuman or degrading treatment of individuals or groups; hardship and injustice brought about by the dominance of one group over another; the negative and demeaning exercise of power. Oppression often involves disregarding the rights of an individual or group and thus is a denial of citizenship'. (Thompson, 2001: 34)

The word 'oppression' means different things to different people. To some, perhaps, it conjures up images of slavery, or apartheid, or medieval despotism, and it may seem to be stretching things to equate the term with the circumstances of most users of social work services, who may be struggling with difficulties of one kind or another, but are not subjected to the slave-driver's whip, or imprisoned for failing to carry a pass, or burnt at the stake for subscribing to the wrong religion. Many service users themselves might object to the word 'oppressed' being applied to them, even if they do feel 'weighed down upon', and there is no reason why we should try (for instance) to describe an elderly couple as oppressed just because they feel the need to ask a social services department to make an assessment of their social care needs.

Nevertheless, a significant proportion of service users – especially in some client groups – are living in inferior housing, on minimal incomes, with little or no work opportunities, minimal education, in an environment where crime is a risk many times higher than the national average. Many belong to groups which are stigmatised and discriminated against. In any social services office you will see people who are very obviously poor and down-trodden. The word 'oppressed' seems to us to be a fair and accurate word to use, though some might prefer 'hard put upon', 'disadvantaged', 'deprived' or 'marginalised'. There are of course more derogatory words than these and we regret to say that if you look in social work files you may come across some of them – 'inadequate' is one particularly unpleasant word that was once quite commonly used in files – a reminder that social work, for all its 'anti-oppressive' rhetoric, is quite capable of being oppressive in its own right.

'Inadequate'

The word 'inadequate' seems to us an appalling word to apply to a human being but it was once in pretty common use among social workers.

What is insidious about a word like inadequate is that it places the responsibility for a person's difficulties entirely within themselves.

Words like 'oppressed' or 'marginalised' have the advantage that they explicitly acknowledge that external circumstances, the way society is structured, the messages we receive about ourselves from others, play a major role in determining what we have to deal with in life, and our capacity to deal with it.

Not all social work service users are economically deprived, of course – some are even wealthy. But all service users belong to groups which are, at least to some extent, in a marginalised position in society: disabled people, people with mental health problems, people with drug and alcohol problems, elderly people, children and parents who are struggling with family life. The problems experienced by all these people are not simply of their own making, but result from the attitudes and responses of society at large. The following exercise illustrates what we mean by this.

Exercise 8.2

When he started secondary school, Danny could still barely read and write. (Neither of Danny's parents could read or write either, so they weren't in a position to help him.) The school was in an area where there were serious problems with recruiting teachers and a chronic shortage of staff, so that a lot of the teaching was done by a constantly changing stream of supply teachers, who tended to be preoccupied with managing difficult behaviour in the classroom, of which there was a lot, rather than teaching. There were a lot of people with problems in the area and it was a neighbourhood with high levels of unemployment and social deprivation. Class sizes were at least 35.

In this context, Danny's literacy problems were not really picked up on, nor was the fact that he never completed homework. He had almost no contact with teachers, just sat at the back of the class waiting for it to finish. Classes were incredibly tedious. The day passed unbearably slowly as he waited for each hour of incomprehensible talk to go by. Classes were also humiliating. They made him feel stupid, which is what some of the other children called him. Danny had always been a bit clumsy and awkward with other children; not a complete loner, but always on the edge of things.

After about a year, he was surprised and flattered to find that a certain group of boys were prepared to take him on as a member of their group. These boys missed a lot of school which at first Danny found shocking, but when they asked him what he got out of school, he had to admit it was absolutely nothing, so he started missing school too. Notes went home to his parents, but nothing else happened.

Danny and his new friends started to miss more and more school and to get involved in increasingly reckless adventures. Pretty soon Danny was involved in vandalism, shoplifting and taking and driving motor vehicles. He started getting caught. He became known to the police. The Youth Offending Team became involved.

Would you describe Danny as oppressed? And if so, why?

Comments on Exercise 8.2

We would definitely describe him as oppressed for the following reasons:

He has now acquired the label of a young offender, a criminal, and yet there is no reason to believe that this was some sort of in-built part of his nature.

The fact is that the educational system failed him. This is not necessarily the fault of individual teachers, but a problem caused by the fact that the school was not adequately resourced to cope in the environment in which it was located. Teachers did not have time to notice Danny as an individual or to pick up on his problems, and as a result school became a tedious, humiliating, pointless ordeal.

In this context it is not surprising that he was attracted to truancy and then to crime. It was a chance to be someone, to feel that he was actually doing something daring and exciting, and not just sitting around feeling like a fool.

The inadequacies of the education system cannot be blamed for 'making him a criminal' – he has to take some responsibility for his choices – but it can certainly blamed for making this choice attractive and for not offering any alternatives that would feel meaningful and allow him his dignity.

In this exercise, we talked about Danny as an individual, but of course the oppression experienced by Danny is likely, to a greater or lesser degree, to be experienced by the entire community in which he lives. There are limited opportunities (high unemployment, high poverty) and the local secondary school is clearly not adequate to the task of meeting the educational needs of its pupils. It is quite likely that other local services will have similar inadequacies.

Oppression isn't just something that happens to certain individuals. It happens to *groups* of one kind or another. Allowing areas of 'deprivation' to develop and failing to provide adequate resources to allow those areas to recover – or their inhabitants to move on – is a way in which society at large oppresses certain sections of the population. In this case the section of the population involved is the inhabitants of a particular neighbourhood as well as the social class to which they belong.

Women, black people and gypsies/travellers are examples of different kinds of group who experience oppression of various kinds in society at large, but who also experience oppression at the hands of social work and other welfare agencies.

Exercise 8.3

Can you think of ways in which a social work agency's behaviour might constitute oppression in relation to:

(Continued)

Exercise 8.3   (Continued)

(a)   people from poor working-class backgrounds
(b)   women
(c)   black people?

Comments on Exercise 8.3

(a)   In the last chapter we suggested that social work and other agencies share confidential information about poor working-class people in a way that would not be tolerated if it was the norm in a prosperous middle-class community.

(b)   Society expects women to be carers, but does not place the same expectations on men. Informal women carers of elderly or disabled people – daughters, wives, daughter-in-laws – may be placed under pressure (remember the primary meaning of 'oppress' as weigh down) to cope with extremely demanding and completely unpaid work in order to save service departments from having to pay for care.

(c)   An example of the way agencies can be oppressive to black people is provided by Thompson (2001) who comments that racism manifests itself in social work through the 'over-representation of black people in "control" situations [Mental Health Act sections, care orders, custodial sentences in criminal cases] and under-representation in "care situations"'. In short: black people are more likely to be subjected to legal coercion than white people.

One danger in recognising that certain groups are oppressed, though, is that we end up thinking of service users – even sentimentalising them – in the passive role of 'victims'. It is therefore important to remember that an oppressed person does not cease to be a moral agent and people who are oppressed may themselves act oppressively. Oppression isn't something that is only practised by the overtly powerful, or by those who hold positions of authority. We all have the potential to be both oppressor and oppressed. Franz Fanon, for instance, asserts 'that at one time we may be oppressed, whereas at another, we may be the oppressor' (Fanon, 1967, cited in Keating, 1997: 10).

Among the most clearly oppressed in society are children living in grossly neglectful or abusive situations. To be in a situation where you are abused but to have no means of escaping from that situation because of the huge power differences between yourself and your abuser, is surely a 'textbook case' of oppression in terms of the two definitions we gave earlier.

The difficulty that social workers often face is that abusive or neglectful parents are often themselves from oppressed groups (though of course by no means always). When this is the case the social worker needs to strike a balance. It is important that she does not let concern to avoid acting oppressively towards the parents blind her to the oppression suffered by the child. But it is equally important that she does not allow her concern to protect the child to provide a pretext for acting oppressively towards the family as a whole, or ignoring the structural oppression which the family may be up against. Not only would this be unjust to the parents, but ultimately it would be unhelpful to the child.

Levels of oppression

Structural oppression

... systems of beliefs, policies, institutions and culture that systematically discriminate against and demean women, black people, people with disabilities, lesbians and gays, working-class people and other oppressed groups. (Banks, 2001: 132)

Structural oppression arises from the way the social system itself is structured. One can make a distinction between structural oppression and the oppressive behaviour of individuals which is not unlike the distinction between *institutional racism* and racist actions by individuals. Indeed institutional racism is an instance of structural oppression.

As we have already noted, it is not simply isolated individuals who are oppressed but groups and in many case the oppression of groups is structural, which is to say that it is built into the way society itself operates, allowing some groups or individuals to make the rules, and others to be excluded.

Keating (1997) offers a multidimensional model, on similar lines to Thompson's 'PCS' model (2001) which we discussed in Chapter 3, to clarify the different levels at which oppression operates. The dimensions, or levels, he proposed are the 'socio-politicial', the 'socio-cultural' and the 'psychological'. The socio-political level is the level at which 'oppression is legitimated and institutionalised' and the level at which power is used to 'dominate and assign differential status to groups' (Keating, 1997: 36). The socio-cultural level is the level at which oppression is transmitted and propagated in society. At this level oppression is mediated through language and the way we 'construct meaning' (ibid.). Keating points in particular to the way in which we define *difference*, which is one of the cornerstones upon which oppression is built. (Consider the ideas and assumptions that have been built up around the term 'asylum seeker' or 'immigrant' in modern British society and you begin to see how this works.) The psychological level refers to the ways in which an individual is affected by oppression and to the ways in which those experiences impact on that individual's life.

The danger is that we either fail to see oppression for what it is at all, or that we see it only at the psychological level, without recognising all its socio-cultural and socio-political underpinnings, in which case we may end up laying responsibility for the psychological effects of oppression upon the affected individual himself or herself, rather than seeing it as a response to external circumstances. Good social work practice therefore requires that social workers:

- are able to recognise the causes of oppression;
- differentiate personal and institutional (or structural) oppression;
- develop insights into the causes of oppression;
- understand the impact of oppression on the lives of service users;
- challenge oppression;
- practise in a way that reduces rather than increases the effects of oppression.

The internalisation of oppression

One of the crueller aspects of the psychology of oppression is the way that the oppressed tend to 'internalise' their own oppression. In fact this internalisation is an important part of the way that an oppressor maintains domination and control. An example is the way in which an abused child who is constantly told she is worthless and deserving only of abuse may herself come to believe this: worthlessness and being deserving of abuse become part of her self-image. But the same sort of process occurs with whole groups who come to believe in the justification for their own oppression. In his autobiography the South African leader, Nelson Mandela, gives a good example of this when he describes his momentary feeling of panic when, on boarding an aeroplane, he noticed that the pilot, like himself, was black:

> We put down briefly in Khartoum where we changed to an Ethiopian Airways flight to Addis. Here I experienced a rather strange sensation. As I was boarding the plane I saw that the pilot was black. I had never seen a black pilot before, and the instant I did I had to quell my panic. How could a black man fly a plane? But a moment later I caught myself: I had fallen into the apartheid mind-set, thinking that Africans were inferior and that flying was a white man's job. (Mandela, 1994: 347–8)

Even though he spent his life fighting the kind of racist attitude that said that black people could not do skilled, responsible jobs like flying airliners, Nelson Mandela had internalised a bit of that attitude himself.

The term 'internalised oppression' refers to exactly this kind of process whereby the oppressed take on and adopt the oppressor's stereotypes. As Freire writes:

> Self-deprecation is another characteristic of the oppressed, which derives from their internalisation of the opinion that oppressors hold of them. So often do they hear that they are good for nothing, know nothing and are incapable of learning anything – that they are sick, lazy and unproductive – that in the end they become convinced of their own unfitness. (Freire, 1993: 45)

One insidious way that social workers can unintentionally feed into the internalised oppression of service users is by encouraging dependency. A person who feels 'good for nothing' can easily be persuaded that it is better to hand over all his problems to someone else to solve, and a social worker who, for whatever reason, is willing to take on a service user's problems (as opposed to supporting the service user in resolving them for himself), is in danger of entrenching this pattern.

Oppression, objectification and 'respect for persons'

> When Israel was in Egypt's land
> Oppressed so hard they could not stand
> Let my people go ...
> (African-American spiritual)

There are two aspects to oppression, both of which are contained in the dictionary definition given earlier: the structural and the personal. On the one hand the word 'oppression' refers to *an unequal power relationship which is abused in the interest of the powerful*. On the other hand 'oppression' refers to the *individual experience of being weighed down and crushed*. To understand how oppression works we need to understand how power operates in society. But to understand why oppression *matters* we need to understand what it does to human beings.

What, in human terms (as opposed to structural ones), do oppressors do to those they oppress? They crush their spirits, they deny them their rights, they deny them their humanity. In fact oppression can be seen as a denial of the 'respect for persons' which is generally seen as fundamental to social work values and those of other caring professions. You will remember that, in Kant's philosophy, what underlay the idea of respect for persons was the 'categorical imperative'. People are ends in themselves, not means to an end. Oppression involves ignoring this fact and uses people as a means to an end.

Perhaps the ultimate case of treating people as means rather than ends is that of slavery, for a slave is treated as an object, a possession to be bought, sold and used for whatever purpose is convenient. Slavery epitomises the process of *objectifying* human beings that is characteristic, to a greater or lesser extent, of all forms of oppression.

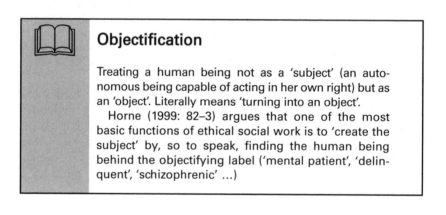

Objectification

Treating a human being not as a 'subject' (an auto-nomous being capable of acting in her own right) but as an 'object'. Literally means 'turning into an object'.

Horne (1999: 82–3) argues that one of the most basic functions of ethical social work is to 'create the subject' by, so to speak, finding the human being behind the objectifying label ('mental patient', 'delin-quent', 'schizophrenic' ...)

Some might consider slavery to be a thing of the past, but unfortunately it is still very much with us. Even in Western countries where liberty is supposedly protected by the law, instances of enslavement regularly occur, particularly of women and girls for sexual purposes, or for use as domestic drudges. But slavery is an extreme case. Oppression also occurs in more insidious, less obvious ways. Unfortunately we can easily find instances of objectification of human beings not only within society at large but *even within social work itself*. This typically occurs in one of two ways:

1   When social work acts as the instrument of policies that have the effect of 'objectifying' people.
2   When social workers and social work agencies 'objectify' human beings to meet their own personal or organisational needs.

The latter can occur in a number of ways and for a number of reasons. When working a great deal with human suffering it is necessary to defend yourself against being overwhelmed by it. When required to do difficult things that will distress people – removing a child from a parent, insisting that an elderly person leave her home – it is necessary to defend oneself against one's own feelings of distress and guilt (even if the action is justified). One way of doing this is to stop seeing the service user as a fellow human being and to start seeing them just as a 'service user', or a 'client', a member, so to speak, of a different species.

It is particularly easy to do this if the service user belongs to a different group from yourself: a different class, a different ethnic group, a different age group ... This is one way in which racism, sexism, classism, ageism (in respect both of old people and of children) and disablism can creep unnoticed into our thinking.

In fact, if you look just at the language that is used in social work offices, it is steeped in terminology that has the effect of objectifying people. Consider the term 'bed blocker' (used to describe patients, usually elderly, who are seen as in need of prompt removal from hospital so as to free up beds). Or the simple word 'case'. Or the use of words like 'intake' to describe teams that deal with new referrals (as if human needs could be processed like some kind of industrial raw material being sucked into a machine)!

It is necessary in social work to find ways of distancing yourself from the distress that often surrounds you, but this means that it is constantly necessary to be aware that you may stopping treating people as people and start treating them as objects: oppressing them, in fact. It is probably particularly easy in respect of people who are not in a position to insist on their own viewpoint being heard, such as small children, but it can happen with service users of all ages.

A simple test, then, that can be used to help answer the question 'Am I acting oppressively?' is: 'Am I treating people with respect: as ends in themselves and not just means?' Our late colleague, David Brandon, said that 'respect is seeing the ... superficiality of positions of moral superiority. The other person is as good as you' (Brandon, 1990: 59).

Oppression and discrimination

We have already noted that we use the term 'anti-oppressive' so frequently in the social work literature as to run the risk that we may stop thinking about what it is supposed to mean. The same applies to the word 'anti-discriminatory'. To make things more difficult, the latter is sometimes used interchangeably with 'anti-oppressive' and at other times as if there was a clear distinction between the two.

Anti-oppressive *and* anti-discriminatory practice

We are offering several accounts of these two terms because different writers do not necessary distinguish the terms in the same way.

From *Anti-Oppressive Practice*
'... anti-oppressive practice is about minimising the power differences in society ... Anti-discriminatory practice uses particular legislation to *challenge* the discrimination faced by some groups of people.

Anti-discriminatory and anti-oppressive practice can complement each other. We do not deny the usefulness of anti-discriminatory practice but we feel that it is limiting in its potential to challenging power differentials. (Dalrymple and Burke, 1995: 3)

From *the Blackwell Encyclopaedia of Social Work*:
Anti-oppressive practice is a radical social work approach which is informed by humanistic and social justice values and takes account of the experiences and views of oppressed people. It is based on an understanding of how the concepts of power, oppression and inequality determine personal and structural relations ...

Anti-discriminatory practice is an approach to social work which emphasises the various ways in which particular individuals and groups tend to be discriminated against and the need for professional practice to counter such discrimination ... (Davies, ed., 2000: 12, 14)

From *Anti-discriminatory Practice* (3rd Edition)
'It has become the practice in recent years for some commentators to distinguish between anti-discriminatory and anti-oppressive practice ... [but] this is not a distinction I shall be drawing here ... Anti-discriminatory and anti-oppressive practice are therefore presented here as more or less synonymous ... (Thompson, 2001: x)

The confusion between the two concepts may lie in the fact that while the words 'oppression' and 'discrimination' certainly mean different things (we will explore discrimination more fully in the next chapter), the two are closely linked in practice:

(a) To discriminate against someone without a valid reason is clearly oppressive. (Banks (2001: 13) gives an example of travellers excluded from a playgroup on the grounds that their presence would upset other parents)

(b) Discriminatory arguments are used to justify oppression.

Slavery and colonialism: oppression justified by discrimination

As we mentioned in Chapter 2, the USA was founded on the idea that it was a self-evident truth that every man had the right to 'life, liberty and the pursuit of happiness'. How then did this nation, of all nations, manage to justify the abduction of millions of human beings from Africa to be bought and sold like chattels in the 'Land of the Free'?

People construct ideological systems to explain and rationalise their own behaviour. The way that belief in human liberty was reconciled with slavery was to discriminate between black and white people, to the point where the black 'race' could be regarded as so inferior to the 'white' that its members could be treated as if they were not fully human. (This was essentially the same process that allowed the Nazis to exterminate millions of Jews and gypsies in the gas chambers on the grounds that they were 'subhuman'; but even larger numbers of Africans died crossing the Atlantic packed into slave ships.)

Spurious discrimination on grounds of skin colour was necessary in order to justify oppression in the form of slavery. It was also necessary to justify the colonial annexation, by Britain, France and other European powers, of countries already inhabited by dark-skinned people. It is useful to remind ourselves that, although racial prejudices of one kind or another have very probably always existed, ideological racism – the *specific* belief in the intrinsic, biological inferiority of some races and the intrinsic biological superiority of the white race – has only existed for the last few hundred years, since the era of slavery and imperialism.

It is also useful – and shocking – to remind ourselves how recently slavery was abolished: 1833 in the British Empire, 1865 in the USA. *There are elderly people still alive today in the USA, Britain and the West Indies who in their childhood could have met old people who had been born into slavery.*

(Continued)

(Continued)

Colonial rule by Britain of dozens of African, Asian and Caribbean countries – a rule that involved rigidly discriminating between white people and 'natives' – ended still more recently, within the memory of any reader of this book who is 40 years old or more. *Apartheid*, which perpetuated the kinds of division between white and black that were normal in the British Empire, was of course dismantled even more recently.

We have given the above account of the historic origins of racism because it is a good example of the way that discrimination can be used to justify oppression. Although it may at first seem at some distance from social work, we believe it is important to remind ourselves how recent this history is because it helps us to understand why racism is very much still with us and in us, both as individuals and as a society, and why as social workers it is essential to take seriously the everyday reality of racism by black and Asian people.

However, it is possible to think of examples which are more recent and closer to home of the ways in which discriminatory thinking can be used to justify oppression.

Exercise 8.4

Can you think of examples that you might encounter in social work or social care, now or in the past, of situations in which oppressive behaviour was justified or rationalised by discriminatory thinking?

Comments on Exercise 8.4

Here are few suggestions:

- Adults with learning disabilities being denied control over their own finances, denied the right to form sexual relationships, or to have privacy in their living accommodation on the grounds that 'they are really just like children'.

- The complete absence of service users from ethnic minorities ...
  the caseload of an adult assessment team is justified on the
  grounds that 'They look after their own'.
- A violent assault on a child is tolerated because 'it is normal in
  their culture'.

People who behave in oppressive ways have to justify to themselves the fact
that they are treating others differently from the way they themselves would
like to be treated. This is much easier to do if they can persuade themselves
that these other people are somehow different from themselves. Both on a
very small scale and on the very large societal scale that justifies slavery and
empire and genocide, the same dynamic is at work. Figure 8.1 illustrates this
oppressive cycle of work and suggests a number of points at which, even if
only in small ways, social workers can try to challenge and interrupt it.

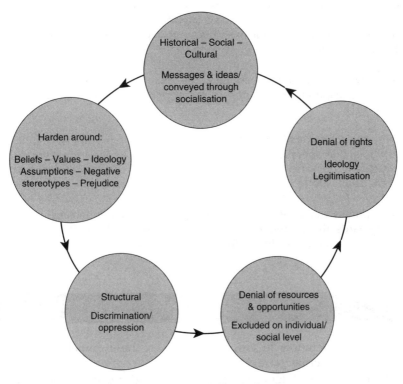

Figure 8.1 The cycle of oppression and discrimination

ounter oppression?

d that social workers can challenge oppression – and
r has been that social workers have an ethical respon-
re is scope for debate as to how much this is really
the following comments on 'anti-oppressive' prac-
...e you to consider in Exercise 8.5:

There is no middle ground; intervention either adds to oppression (or at least condones it) or goes some small way towards easing or breaking such oppression. In this respect, the political slogan, 'If you're not part of the solution you're part of the problem' is probably accurate. An awareness of the sociopolitical context is necessary in order to prevent becoming (or remaining) part of the problem. (Thompson, 1992: 169–70)

The rhetoric of anti-oppressive practice is generally couched in terms of challenging structural oppression ... Yet as this rhetoric is incorporated into mainstream practice, it is questionable sometimes whether 'empowerment' and 'anti-oppressive practice' consist of anything more than enabling individual users to gain confidence and offering 'individually sensitive practice' that takes into account, for example, a user's dietary and religious needs. (Banks, 2001: 132)

Social workers should not confuse the reality of the actual effect of their work with aspirations captured in mere politically correct slogans. (Clark, 2000: 161)

Many social workers believe that policies in welfare are unjust both in conception and in operation ... Ignoring injustice in the spheres that social work particularly operates in cannot meet the requirements of ethical practice. (Clark, 2000: 199)

Anti-oppressive practice ... means recognising power imbalances and working towards the promotion of change to redress the balance of power. (Dalrymple and Burke, 1995: 15)

Exercise 8.5

There are differences in emphasis between these quotations. How would you describe those differences?

Which of these statements do you agree with most, and which do you disagree with? Why?

Comments on Exercise 8.5

The main difference in emphasis we notice between these five quotations is as follows:

Thompson, and Dalrymple and Burke, regard challenging and trying to overturn structural oppression as central to social work practice. The quote from Banks and the first quote from Clark, on the other hand, seem more sceptical about social work's ability to make real changes in structural terms and suggest that, in practice, talk of anti-oppressive practice may be little more than lip service. The second quote from Clark is however clear that to collude in injustice and oppression is unethical.

It would surely be a fallacy to suppose that social workers – acting in their professional capacity – could bring about a structural change in society. (Who knows what they could do acting as part of a political party or a campaigning movement, but that is another story.) Almost all social workers, after all, are either employed by the state or employed by voluntary agencies which are partly funded by the state. And social workers are not paid to do what they like, but to deliver specific services of various kinds on behalf of their state- and voluntary-sector employers.

It is also a mistake to believe that tackling structural oppression is the only useful thing a social worker can do. Most social workers most of the time are delivering services which, at best, are *useful* to people, just as bank managers, doctors and accountants do, along with plumbers, builders, electricians and those who carry out countless other useful activities. We can be useful without changing the world.

But social workers *are* in a position where (a) they can very easily add to the oppression experienced by some members of society, (b) they can, however also often do something to assist individuals – and sometimes groups – to take back some power for themselves.

To oppress someone is to deny them respect. Therefore, although social workers cannot change the world, they and other professionals, do have an ethical responsibility:

- to avoid behaving in an oppressive way, or adding to the oppression of those who are already oppressed. (Behaving in an oppressive way would include undermining people, denying them the right to their own view and their own perspective, acting in such a way as to diminish their self-esteem, restricting their liberty without good cause, doing something for them that they could do themselves);

- to try as far as possible to empower service users to take more control over their own lives;
- to refuse to collude in policies that they believe are oppressive in effect.

The last point opens up the possibility of entering into conflict with employers, and this carries risks for social workers themselves, but to fail to challenge policies which you sincerely believe are oppressive is to abdicate responsibility for your own ethical conduct. (In the Nuremberg trials after World War II, some Nazi war criminals tried to excuse their actions by saying, 'We were only obeying orders!' Quite rightly this was not accepted as a defence.)

Minimum intervention/maximum partnership

So whatever the limitations of social work as a political force, social workers can and should act in a way that avoids adding to oppression and gives people support in challenging oppression that they face. We will conclude this chapter by drawing your attention to some simple but crucial principles of 'anti-oppressive' practice which we have partly taken from Jane Dalrymple and Beverley Burke (1995): the principle of *minimal intervention* and the principle of *maximising partnership*.

Minimising intervention

Any social work intervention is an intrusion, however well meant and however much it is welcomed, into the privacy of an individual's or a family's life. Most social workers are acting as agents of the state, which means that (whether they like it or not) their encounters with service users are based on a gigantic power imbalance. All social workers represent, and have the backing of, organisations, so that even in the non-statutory sector the power imbalance is still very much present. Dalrymple and Burke go so far as to say that 'the use of the word intervention is oppressive and by its very nature indicates where the power base lies' (Dalrymple and Burke, 1995: 89). We would agree with them, though we do not think we can change anything simply by changing the word.

It is therefore important for social workers not to think of intervention as necessarily a 'good thing', even if well meant. On the contrary it is something to be avoided unless (a) it is clearly requested by the service user and/or is clearly required for the protection of others who are not in a position to protect themselves, and (b) there are strong indications that it is needed and good reasons to believe that it would be helpful. Simply to intervene in order to prove that you 'tried to do something' is not good practice.

When social workers do intervene, the intervention should be the minimum, and the least intrusive, required to achieve the goal. Intervention should only be either at the request of the service user, or *on the basis of a clear statutory mandate* (such as Section 37 of the 1989 Children Act or Section 2 of the 1983 Mental Health Act). Visiting a household without a clear request to do so is only appropriate under such a mandate. Whether visiting on request or under a statutory mandate, it is always important to be clear – and as far as possible to agree – why you are there, and what are the rules, limits and timescale of your involvement.

Maximising partnership

'Partnership' is a much over-used word in social work, and often means next to nothing, so we are a little hesitant to use it here. The reality is that a true partnership cannot exist when there is a grossly unequal distribution of power. For this reason it seems to us inappropriate to talk about 'working in partnership' when, for instance, parents are having to comply with a plan drawn up by a social worker in order to have their children's names removed from the child protection register.

However, the fact that we cannot do everything should never be a pretext for doing nothing. There are many ways in which social workers can reduce the sense of intervention as being something 'done to' a service user and make it into something which is 'done with', 'on behalf of' or 'in consultation with' the service user. Here are a few suggestions:

- Explaining to service users how you record your work with them and providing them with copies of your records. Or jointly discussing how your meetings with them are to be recorded.
- Not consulting other professionals about the service user, or passing on information about the service user, without the service user's permission and knowledge. Or, in situations where it has to be done anyway, at least informing the service user in advance about the nature and extent of information-sharing that will go on.
- Inviting the service user to give her own explanations of what is going on in her life and being extremely wary of offering your own explanations.
- Asking service users how they wish to be addressed, and not simply calling people by their first names.
- Being clear about your role and the boundaries of your role.
- Being clear and honest about the purpose of your involvement and not using devious means to 'make things easier' for the service user or yourself (i.e. if you are visiting to check up on them, say so; do not pretend you are there for some other purpose).
- Not using jargon, or explaining it properly if you have to use it.

All of these points really add up to treating service users as we would wish and expect to be treated by professionals: with respect.

Chapter summary

This chapter has considered the idea of oppression, looking at both the ways in which social workers may encounter it and the ways in which social workers may themselves cause it. We have suggested that the antithesis of oppression is the basic value of respect. We have discussed the extent to which social work can impact on structural oppression.

The topics covered have been:

- What is oppression?
- Levels of oppression
- The internalisation of oppression
- Oppression, objectification and 'respect for persons'
- Oppression and discrimination
- Can social work counter oppression?
- Minimum intervention/maximum partnership

 **9** # Difference and Diversity

---

- Differences, diversity and discrimination
- Being discriminating and being discriminatory
- Dimensions of difference

  - ➢ Ethnicity/race
  - ➢ Class
  - ➢ Gender
  - ➢ Disability
  - ➢ Age

- The benefits of difference and diversity

This chapter will consider some of the implications of the fact that every human society has to deal with difference and diversity – differences in ability, differences in appearance, differences in cultural practices and beliefs, differences in gender and sexual orientation – and will look at the ways that many kinds of difference are used as a pretext for discrimination and oppression.

A good starting point here is to consider your own experiences of being *different*. If you are disabled, or are a member of an ethnic minority in your own country, or are gay, you will have had rather more experience of this than some readers, but everyone will at some point have found themselves in a position where they feel different from those around them:

Exercise 9.1

Consider the following situations:

- You are visiting a city and manage to get completely lost. In the part of the city where you find yourself, you become aware that you are

(Continued)

Exercise 9.1   (Continued)

the only person on the street who looks the way you do (you are the only white person, or the only black person). You are surrounded by people who look different from you and speak to one another in a language you don't understand. You need help in finding your way back to where you started from.

- You are invited to a formal occasion – a wedding perhaps, or a funeral. When you get there, you realise that you have not understood the dress code for the occasion. You are dressed completely differently from everyone else.

- You find yourself in a social gathering where everyone else present is a member of a different social class from yourself (you are the only working-class person at a party of middle-class people, perhaps, or vice versa).

- You are the only man in a gathering of women – or the only woman in a gathering of men.

(Or, if you can think of better examples of situations where you were aware of being *different*, think about those.)

What feelings come up in situations such as these? How do you react? What strategies do you adopt?

Comments on Exercise 9.1

These types of situation, where you find yourself in a minority, surrounded by people who are recognisably different to yourself, have, at the very least, the potential to be uncomfortable. We often fear ridicule or rejection or being the subject of unwelcome attention. Many readers of this book may have had at least some experience of being in situations of this kind and fearing for their physical safety. Sometimes those fears may have been justified. There really are situations where simply being different places us in physical – even mortal – danger. Sometimes those fears have not been justified but we feel them nevertheless.

As we have already observed, everyone has these experiences – no one can go through life feeling all the time that they are part of the majority – but some groups of people are placed in these situations much more often than others. Of the authors of this book, for instance, Andrew – as a black man living in a country which is more than 90 per cent white – will obviously far more frequently have experiences of this kind than a white man such as Chris. For those who have such experiences less often, imagination is called for in appreciating the position of those who do.

As to how we react, there seem to be a number of possibilities. Sometimes people try and hide their differences (consider gay people who choose not to disclose the fact that they are gay), or minimise them, or even try to 'curry favour' with the majority group (consider the way that some men in a predominantly female context – such as a social work office – make self-deprecating remarks about men in an effort to identify themselves as different from other men). Sometimes people react defensively, become prickly and hostile and even exaggerate their differences (consider the way that some working-class people in a middle-class context feel the need to exaggerate their working-class accent in order to emphasise their difference from those around them.)

This exercise demonstrates, we hope, that whether we like it or not, being different can be difficult and that it really makes a difference to us whether we feel the same as or different to those around us. In the exercise we considered the experience of being in a minority and the fact that it feels uncomfortable. Perhaps a second exercise will help to illustrate just *why* it feels uncomfortable. We suspect that this exercise is probably also rather more uncomfortable to do.

Exercise 9.2

Being as honest with yourself as you can be, try and think of one thing that you sometimes find yourself disliking or being annoyed or irritated by, about the following:

- People of the opposite gender to yourself
- Old people – or young people if you consider yourself to be old
- People with disabilities – or people with different disabilities to yourself
- People who belong to a different ethnic group to yourself
- People from a different social class

> ## Comments on Exercise 9.2
>
> We suspect that most people will not have had much difficulty in think-ing of something that they dislike or are irritated by in each of these categories. If we are honest with ourselves, it is not so difficult to see how these minor dislikes and irritations can, under certain circum-stances, grow into something more sinister: hostility and even hatred.

Differences, diversity and discrimination

It is a fact of human existence that everyone's experience is unique. No one can know exactly what it feels like to be another person. This is at the same time useful ('horses for courses', as the saying goes), fascinating, exasperat-ing, a threat, exciting, lonely, a source of comfort and a source of oppression and cruelty. The difference between the sexes, for instance, is often the basis for love, attraction and fascination, but a huge source too of misunderstand-ings, assumptions, exasperation and pain. And it has been the basis of all sorts of unfair discrimination and cruel oppression.

The existence of difference is a challenge to our own identity. If someone makes different choices to me, does that mean my choices are wrong? If someone believes in a different god to me, aren't they calling my god into question? If someone speaks a different language, how can I be sure of what they are saying? And the same insecurities can arise when people look dif-ferent, or have a different kind of body or different sexual interests.

And since difference can feel like a threat, there is always a certain temp-tation to exclude those who seem different to ourselves. One of the forms this can take is that of excluding those we think of as different from the rules of conduct that we would want to apply to ourselves.

This can happen at an individual level – *John fails to listen to Susan's point of view because she is a woman, Lucy doesn't notice Michael because he is disabled, Roger discounts Tommy's opinion because he is only a child, Philip discounts Roland's views and feelings because Roland is black.* In all kinds of circumstances one person may discount the views and feelings of others because of some perceived difference.

But it can also happen at the structural level. Groups and categories of human beings can be excluded explicitly (as in apartheid South Africa) or implicitly (as in modern Britain) from full participation in society. Oppression and discrimination at the structural level in turn feed back into individual acts of discrimination (in a vicious circle like that illustrated in Figure 8.1 in the previous chapter): *John might be more inclined to ignore Susan's point of view on political matters if he lived in a society – such as Britain until 1928 – where women were not entitled to vote in elections on the grounds that politics were not for women …*

Dealing with difference is an issue for all of us at an individual level. It is an issue for society at a structural level. And we as individuals have to operate within a society and a culture which includes ideas and assumptions about different groups of people. For these reasons any discussion about values and ethics needs to include some reflection on the issues raised by the fact of difference and diversity.

Being discriminating and being discriminatory

Discrimination etc.

Discriminate – 'be, set up, or act on the basis of, a difference … ; make a distinction, esp. unjustly on grounds of race or colour or sex; … observe distinctions carefully, have good judgement …' (*Concise Oxford Dictionary*, 7th Edition, 1982)

So the word has a neutral meaning ('act on the basis of a difference'), a negative meaning ('make a distinction unjustly') and a positive meaning ('have good' judgement').

Discriminatory has the purely negative meaning of discriminating unfairly.

Positive discrimination is a term used to describe acts of discrimination intended to have desirable consequences for a group which has been discriminated against, for instance reserving certain jobs for people from ethnic minorities who are under-represented in the workforce.

The word 'discrimination' is a somewhat confusing one. We need to be clear that discrimination is part of a social worker's job. Social workers *need* to discriminate between one person and another – taking into account a whole range of factors including class and culture, as well as individual life history – if they are to provide a good service tailored to an individual's needs. In the real world of limited resources and time, it is necessary to discriminate in order to decide who gets a service now, who will have to wait and who can't have a service from your agency at all. As Neil Thompson puts it, 'to discriminate, in its general sense, is an essential part of social interaction, and indeed of making sense of our lives' (Thompson, 2002: 43). It is not wrong *per se* to treat one person differently to another.

When we talk about anti-discriminatory practice, therefore, we are talking about practice aimed at countering not discrimination itself, but discrimination that is unfair, unjust and unwarranted. For a nursery school to use age as criterion of admission is not unwarranted, since the nursery school has a specific brief to meet the needs of a certain age group. For it to use ethnic origin as a criterion *would* be unwarranted – and in fact would also be illegal in the UK under a series of laws dating back to the 1965 Race Relations Act.

For a white foster carer to be given special help in caring for the hair of black foster children, but not to seek the same help for white foster children, is not unwarranted discrimination but a reflection of her own limitations and of the fact that different children have different needs. For her to show favouritism and give preferential treatment to white children over black ones (or vice versa), or boys over girls (or vice versa), *would be* unwarranted discrimination.

Recognising diversity and responding to difference – in face-to-face work and in the planning of services – is good practice. In fact, this is necessary if we are genuinely to show 'respect for others'. Using difference as a basis for providing a preferential service to some groups is bad practice, contrary to the principle of respect for others, and contrary to social justice.

Quotes from the codes of practice

'Social workers have a duty to ... show respect for all persons, and respect service users' beliefs, values, culture, goals, needs, preferences, relationships and affiliations ...' (BASW, 2002: 2)

Social care workers must challenge 'dangerous, abusive, discriminatory or exploitative behaviour and [use] established processes and procedures to report it.' (GSCC, 2002: 3)

'Social workers have a duty to ... ensure that they do not act out of prejudice against any person or group, on any grounds, including origin, ethnicity, class, status, sex, sexual orientation, age, disability, beliefs or contribution to society ...' (BASW, 2002: 4)

Social care workers must not 'discriminate unlawfully against service users, carers or colleagues for any reason or condone any such discrimination on their part' (GSCC, 2002: 4)

'Social workers have a duty to recognise and respect ethnic and cultural identity and diversity, and the further diversity within ethnic and cultural groups, and promote policies, procedures and practices consistent with this objective ...' (BASW, 2002: 4)

Dimensions of difference

People differ from one another in literally countless ways, any one of which has the potential to be a basis of discrimination. Even hair colour, for instance, is the basis of certain stereotypical assumptions that are made about 'blondes' and 'redheads' – 'dumb blondes', 'fiery redheads' – both of which can be burdensome for people with blonde or red hair. However, we will now look at dimensions of difference where unfair discrimination has a strong structural and historic component, and is therefore something that occurs systematically. In all of these dimensions, discriminatory assumptions are so widespread that we can take it as a virtual certainty that we actually hold some of those assumptions ourselves, whether we want to or not. It may be helpful to start by considering your own position.

Exercise 9.3

The 'dimensions of difference', which we are now about to discuss, are

- ethnicity/race
- class
- gender
- disability and
- age

A small part of your own individual identity is measurable along these dimensions. (You must have an age, a gender, and an ethnic background. You will have ideas about your class background. You may or may not have a disability or disabilities.)

You will also have personal circumstances which affect the way you see others who are different from you. You might have a sibling or a child who is disabled, for instance. You might have a close friend who has a different ethnic background to yourself.

You may also feel that there are other 'dimensions' which are very important to your identity but which we have not mentioned here. You may be gay or lesbian. Or you may have suffered from a mental illness and feel that marks you out, in some senses, as different from other people. You may have religious beliefs which are an important part of your sense of self.

(Continued)

Exercise 9.3   (Continued)

What we would like you to do is to reflect on how you are located on these various dimensions – both the ones we have listed and the others which are important to you – and consider how you relate to others who are differently located. (If you are black, how do you relate to people who are white, for instance? If you are not disabled, how do you relate to people who are?)

Along which of these dimensions do you think you find it most difficult to empathise with people who are different from you? Alternatively, are there any of these dimensions in which you feel more comfortable with those who are 'different' than you do with those who are the 'same'?

Comments on Exercise 9.3

Social workers do not give service users justice if they assume that their own particular perspective, based on their own limited life experience, is somehow the right one. For instance, a white person may have difficulty in really understanding what it means to be a black person on the receiving end of racism, and therefore may be inclined to dismiss it as not a serious problem, but this would be a failure to respect the experiences of others. It is important to notice and make allowances for our own 'blind spots', and to notice the areas in which we are most comfortable with difference.

Ethnicity/race

Racism – and 'New Racism'

Many definitions of racism could be offered, not all of which completely agree with each other. Our suggestion is:

> Ideology based on the proposition that a certain ethnic group is superior in worth to others.

> **(Continued)**
>
> Historically, racism was based on alleged biological differences between the races, making some races allegedly inherently inferior to others. But as Clark (2003) points out, there has been a subtle shift in racist ideology. The 'New Racism' relies less on alleged *biological* differences but concentrates instead on 'cultural differences in which the Other becomes demonised' (Clark, 2003: 28). Indeed, New Racist ideologues may actually claim not to *be* racist, but merely to be concerned to protect their culture.

There are visible differences between human beings whose ancestors originated in different parts of the world, and there are also differences in beliefs, language, customs and norms of day to day behaviour. In any situation where people from different ethnic backgrounds live alongside one another, there is the potential for prejudice, conflict and for the oppression of one group by another. Anti-semitism and hostility towards gypsies are examples of prejudices which are still widespread, and both of which, only a little over half a century ago, were used by the Nazis as a pretext for mass murder.

In the huge movements of peoples that took place during the colonial and post-colonial eras literally hundreds of millions of people were transplanted across the globe as a result of colonial conquest, slavery and mass migration. A consequence of this is that most Western countries are multicultural to a greater extent than ever before. People in Western countries have had to become accustomed to living alongside people who look different and have different traditions and beliefs. Since, as we have seen, difference is always a challenge and is often, for various reasons, experienced as a threat, creating a harmonious multicultural and multiracial society presents us with many challenges. Even within a marriage, after all, or between the members of a family, difference presents us with challenges and can be the cause of conflict.

Difference is always difficult, but the prejudices that exist in predominantly white countries about black people and Asian people have a number of specific features:

- Black and Asian people are visibly recognisable as different from the majority population (unlike, say, people of Polish descent). Malcolm Payne comments: 'I am white and grew up without meeting any black people until my late teens. I find it hard not to think of being white as normal and of being black as out of the ordinary' (Payne, 1997: 245).

- In the UK and Europe, black and Asian people continue to be widely seen as incomers (even though their families may have lived in Britain for several generations). As Lena Dominelli puts it: 'White people's right to be in Britain is not being questioned; white people belong here. Black people do not; they are guests' (Dominelli, 1997: 45).
- Black and Asian people face not just the ignorant prejudices which tend to be faced by any recognisably different group, but the very particular ideology of racism – the belief in the intrinsic inferiority of non-white people which, as we discussed earlier, provided the rationale for slavery and colonial rule in Africa and Asia.

Although racism is no longer an officially sanctioned ideology (in the UK and other countries, racial discrimination is against the law), it has had a huge and pervasive influence on our culture. This means that as individual social workers – black and white – we all hold assumptions we are not necessarily aware of, which are likely to affect our practice and decision-making about black and Asian service users in particular. These kinds of assumption also permeate the institutions and structures of our society, in the form of institutional racism.

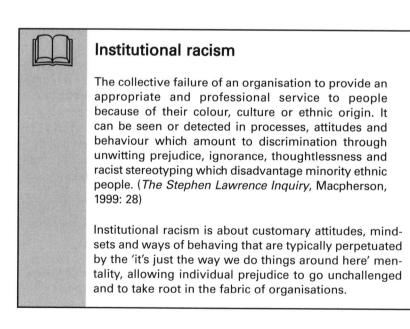

Institutional racism

The collective failure of an organisation to provide an appropriate and professional service to people because of their colour, culture or ethnic origin. It can be seen or detected in processes, attitudes and behaviour which amount to discrimination through unwitting prejudice, ignorance, thoughtlessness and racist stereotyping which disadvantage minority ethnic people. (*The Stephen Lawrence Inquiry*, Macpherson, 1999: 28)

Institutional racism is about customary attitudes, mind-sets and ways of behaving that are typically perpetuated by the 'it's just the way we do things around here' mentality, allowing individual prejudice to go unchallenged and to take root in the fabric of organisations.

Because of the structural character of racism it is not sufficient simply for the social worker to be 'colour-blind' when dealing with her service users, since that entails also being 'blind' to much of the users' experience. Some people have difficulties with this, and feel that it runs contrary to the principle of respect for all persons, as Sarah Banks, for example, illustrates:

> While the 'respect for persons' doctrine would entail that a user who was black ... should be treated as an individual with rights, choices and desires, with no prejudgements or prejudice based on irrelevant factors like skin colour, it would, in effect be a 'colour-blind' approach. For being black would be regarded as irrelevant, whereas the position adopted by anti-racist social workers would be to regard being black as relevant, to see the user as a member of an oppressed group and to take this into account in the social work relationship. (Banks, 2001: 58)

Respect for persons must surely involve a willingness to take into account every aspect of a person's experience and circumstances, including their position in relation to the rest of society. And since we live in a society where a person's skin colour makes a difference to how people are treated, we can't ignore skin colour when considering people's needs. Respect for persons requires that we are *not* colour-blind, at least in a society where racism still exists.

Exercise 9.4

You are a residential social worker in an assessment unit for adolescents. Most of your residents are white, some are black. The black residents are coming in for some bullying from some of the white ones, and this includes racial abuse.

What would be a 'colour-blind' way of dealing with this?

What would be a way of dealing with this that took into account that the recipients of the bullying were 'members of an oppressed group'?

Comments on Exercise 9.4

You may well have more ideas than we have about how to deal with such behaviour in a residential establishment. However, we would suggest that either approach should involve trying to deal with the bullying, perhaps by making arrangements to support and protect the victims and by challenging the bullies, perhaps by imposing restrictions or sanctions on them, or perhaps by trying to work with the residents as a group to find their own solutions.

A 'colour-blind' approach would involve dealing with the bullying as bullying, and name-calling as name-calling, without paying attention to its specifically racist content or to the fact that its victims are exclusively black and its perpetrators exclusively white.

The alternative, anti-racist, approach would recognise that racism was as much of an issue here as bullying and therefore needed tackling as a distinct and separate issue. By putting racist name-calling on a par with other kinds of name-calling, the colour-blind approach is ignoring the fact that racist abuse is not just a personal thing between two groups of boys but part of a pervasive pattern in which a black minority is given negative and threatening messages by a white majority. So the anti-racist approach would need to give a strong message about the unacceptability of bullying behaviour in general and of racism in particular.

As for putting it to the whole residents group as a problem to solve, this would clearly be inappropriate if the residents group, in which white children are in the majority, was polarised further into 'them and us', white and black. The black residents would then find themselves in a position of being outnumbered and might fear that other non-bullying white residents might side with the bullies rather than themselves, or at least be inclined to minimise the bullies' activities. There is also a danger that those not involved might consider they too were being blamed as the perpetrators and join the others in the bullying behaviour.

Class

Classification of social classes

1. Higher managerial and professional occupations
2. Lower managerial and professional occupations
3. Intermediate occupations
4. Small employers and own account workers
5. Lower supervisory, craft and related occupations
6. Semi-routine occupations
7. Routine occupations
8. Never had paid work/long-term unemployed

(Office for National Statistics, 1999)

Curiously, class is very often forgotten in discussions about difference and anti-discriminatory practice. Neil Thompson's *Anti-discriminatory Practice* (2001), for instance, includes chapters on gender, ethnicity, age and disability, but none on class.

Britain is said to be a particularly class-conscious society as compared to North America, Australasia or continental Europe, and some of the following discussion may be less relevant outside the UK. Certainly in British society the social class of a person, like their ethnic origin, is something that we deduce (at times mistakenly) from a whole range of cues including dress, body language, consumer choices – such as choice of newspaper or home décor or clothes – and accent. Working-class people in England, for instance, tend to speak with regional accents which not only identify their class but also roughly which part of the country they come from. Middle-class people – and certainly those who come from established middle-class families – characteristically speak a form of English which linguists know as RP (Received Pronunciation). There are regional variations within RP but they are not very pronounced, with the result that it is often hard to place the geographical origin of an RP speaker. But, while we cannot necessarily place an RP speaker geographically, we do in British society tend to assume that an RP speaker is well educated and belongs to the middle class. It is significant that this accent is commonly referred to as 'posh' and someone with such an accent as 'well-spoken' (as if someone with a working-class accent was 'badly spoken'!)

In the UK, the RP accent is associated with people in powerful, prominent positions: doctors, teachers, judges, politicians, television announcers, clergymen, senior businessmen. It is so rarely associated with people doing low-paid or menial tasks that if we heard, say, a street cleaner talking in an RP accent we would instantly notice it, just as we would instantly notice a prominent judge speaking in a broad regional accent. In other words, RP is associated with power and privilege.

We suggest that if you speak with an RP accent and work in a field such as children and family social work, whose service users tend to come predominantly from poor and/or working-class backgrounds, then the way you speak will be noted as an indicator of difference and a reminder of your powerful position. Even if you *don't* speak with an RP accent, other cues such as your dress and even just the fact that you are a social worker will be read in this way.

You too (we suggest) will inevitably be aware of class differences, just as you will be aware of difference when working with people from a different ethnic background to yourself. There are real dangers of stereotyping people on the basis of the fact that they are of a different class to yourself, or of giving preferential treatment to those you recognise as having a similar background because you find it easier to identify with their situation.

We have many times heard social workers and social work students comment that they are more self-conscious and careful about their practice when dealing with middle-class service users because they are aware that middle-class people tend to be more confident about asserting their rights. This gives some indication of how much social workers normally feel protected by the fact of their powerful position and their social status when they are dealing with poor or working-class families.

It's important to bear in mind too that different classes, like different ethnic groups, have their own cultures and different priorities. Shor (2000), for instance, shows how families from different neighbourhoods have different views about what constitutes child maltreatment.

 Stereotypes

'… a widely held but fixed and oversimplified idea of a particular type of person or thing … .' (*New Oxford Dictionary of English*, Revised Edition 2001)

A stereotype is a form of generalisation. Generalisations are normal and necessary to learning. For example, a child who touches something hot avoids burning herself by generalising this experience to other similar experiences.

However, generalisations about different groups of human beings, even if they have some basis in fact (which is often not the case) are dangerous because they have the effect of shutting us off from contrary experience. If we are convinced that all young men are criminals, for instance, we will tend not to notice or to discount evidence to the contrary.

The effect of this can be deeply oppressive for the person on the receiving end, who is denied the option of being accepted for who they actually are.

Making guesses, and forming hypotheses about other people, is something that we inevitably do. It is when these guesses and hypotheses acquire a sense of permanency and resistance to change that they become stereotypes: the basis upon which labels are attached and from which generalisations are made and sustained.

Gender

Each one of the 'dimensions of difference' we are discussing has its own distinctive characteristics which mean that it cannot be regarded as exactly comparable to the others. What is different about gender, as compared to ethnicity and class, is that men and women do not, on the whole, live in separate communities and separate dwellings. Most households include both men and women. Most of us have men and women among the people we most care about. All of us have both a mother and a father. And if we are parents, whether fathers or mothers, we may have sons or daughters or both, and usually love all of them. (We don't dispute that many people have friends and loved ones from different class and ethnic backgrounds: we just make the point that many people don't!)

But in spite of the close proximity between men and women and the many close ties that cross the gender line, this dimension of difference is, as we know, the source of unwarranted discrimination and real oppression.

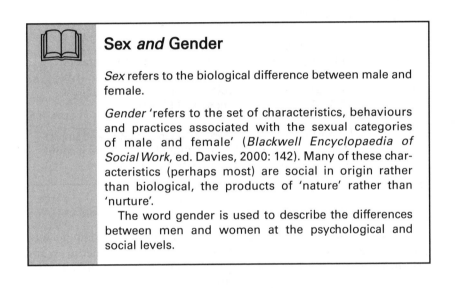

Sex *and* Gender

Sex refers to the biological difference between male and female.

Gender 'refers to the set of characteristics, behaviours and practices associated with the sexual categories of male and female' (*Blackwell Encyclopaedia of Social Work*, ed. Davies, 2000: 142). Many of these characteristics (perhaps most) are social in origin rather than biological, the products of 'nature' rather than 'nurture'.

The word gender is used to describe the differences between men and women at the psychological and social levels.

Both men and women suffer as a result of the restricted roles and expectations to which socially constructed ideas about gender consign them. However, there is no doubt that the most obvious victims of sexism are women. Women are paid less than men, are under-represented at, or absent from, the senior levels of most organisations (including social services departments), and are over-represented in low-paid low-status work such as, in the social care context, that of care assistants.

Women also do more housework than men. A cultural expectation exists (in, as far as we are aware, all cultures) that woman have a particular responsibility for the care of children and of other relatives such as frail elderly parents, or adults with disabilities, with the result that women face much more pressure than men do to make this their priority (consider the judgement that society makes of a woman who walks out on her children, as compared to the judgement that society makes about a man who does so). They are overwhelmingly the main victims of rape and sexual assault and may face humiliation and disbelief in a male-dominated court system if they try and bring their attackers to justice. They are the main victims of domestic violence. It is possible to think of contexts in which men may feel disadvantaged or excluded, but these tend to be at the cultural and individual level, while discrimination against women exists at the institutional or structural level.

Sexism

... a deep-rooted, often unconscious set of beliefs, attitudes and institutions in which distinctions between people's intrinsic worth are made on the grounds of their sex and sexual roles. (Bullock and Stallybrass, 1977: 571, cited by Thompson, 2001: 41)

In practice the word refers to the inequitable and unjust treatment of women by men, though in principle it could refer to unjust treatment of men by women.

Social work is in an interesting position in relation to sexism because it operates in the 'caring' sphere, which is traditionally assigned to women. In Britain the majority of social workers, like nurses, are women, though in senior social work management the genders are reversed. Although social workers deal with men, women, boys and girls as service users, the *carers of others* that they deal with are predominantly women. As representatives of a state welfare system which does not provide care on demand to any user group, but rations it tightly on the basis of need, social workers will often find themselves in the position of trying to encourage women carers to 'hang in there' in the absence of a viable alternative.

This can put social workers on the horns of a dilemma in which, in order to protect the interests of their service user as best they can, they may have to effectively exploit women by prevailing on their goodwill or their conscience. The example in the following exercise illustrates this.

Exercise 9.5

Aged 46, the youngest of four, and the only girl, in a suburban white British family, Sue grew up with parents who pushed their sons to achieve and seemed to value their daughter's achievements very little. Sue didn't leave home until the age of 24 when she married an older man and became a housewife and mother. Her children have both now grown up and left home and she has recently started a job as a learning support assistant in a local school, her first paid work since before she married, which she very much enjoys.

But her mother has now suddenly died and her father, Mr Roberts, suffers from advanced Parkinson's disease. He is in need of daily personal care. Sue's three brothers expect Sue to give up her part-time job to care for him, pointing out that all three of them are the main breadwinners for their families, while Sue's income is small and she is supported financially by her husband. The only alternative is for Mr Roberts to go into a residential home and it is agreed between Sue and her brothers that this would literally kill him, as he is a fiercely independent man who would hate institutional care.

Sue agrees with her brothers about her duty, but the prospect fills her with such dread that she can't sleep at nights and has asked her GP for sleeping pills.

You are the care co-ordinator (social worker) for Mr Roberts. You know that your agency will not be able to fund sufficient domiciliary care to keep Mr Roberts at home without additional input from Sue. His care needs are such that a complete domiciliary care package would actually be more costly than residential care. So residential care is the only alternative.

What would you do?

Comments on Exercise 9.5

In a real life situation of this kind you might well feel that you were left with no option but to leave the burden of decision on the shoulders of Sue, in essence giving her the message:

'Either let your father go into residential care and be blamed by your brothers and yourself for his subsequent deterioration, or once again give up the possibility of a career of your own to provide care for your family!'

As care co-ordinator for Mr Roberts your primary responsibility is for him as service user, but you do also have legal duties to assess Sue's needs as a carer under the 1995 Carers (Recognition and Services) Act. Unfortunately this does not necessarily mean your agency is going to be able to meet those needs.

Perhaps, though, there is a way of challenging the assumptions of Sue's brothers that this is all down to her? Perhaps you could call a family conference, enlisting the GP's help to underline concerns about Sue's health, and pushing for a solution in which all family members contribute time and/or money to add to whatever help your agency is able to give?

The example in the exercise shows, as is so often the case in social work, that it may sometimes be possible to mitigate the effects of oppression, but it is seldom possible to remove the oppression itself – at least not within the narrow confines of the casework relationship and the role that is defined for you by your employers.

Disability

Disablism

'... systematic discrimination and prejudice against people with disabilities which produces a milieu of oppression and degradation' (Thompson, 2001: 111).

We live in what can be described as a disabling society in that people who have physical, sensory or learning impairments of one kind or another are frequently denied access to many of the things other people casually take for granted. The ways in which access is restricted vary from physical obstacles, such as stairs and doorways that cannot be used by people in wheelchairs, to discrimination in selection processes such as job interviews, to a more subtle and pervasive message that comes from public attitudes encountered on the streets and in the media.

Social workers supporting people with learning, physical and sensory disabilities will be very aware of the difficulties that disabled people typically face to achieve many things in life that non-disabled people would regard as normal. Historically these difficulties would have been seen as sad consequences of the individual's impairments and the social worker could be seen as reflecting society's benevolent wish to 'help' these 'unfortunate' people.

In recent times, some disabled people have challenged this way of seeing things and effectively turned it on its head, pointing out that their lack of access to work, public buildings, public transport and so on is not an inevitable consequence of, say, being blind or having non-functioning legs, but is the result of the rest of society failing to make access possible. On this argument, disability is a social construction, a particular way in which society responds to people with impairments. Far from expressing society's benevolence, the services that are made available to disabled people represent crumbs thrown from a table to which disabled people should rightfully have full access.

In this new analysis 'disability is defined as a form of social exclusion and oppression. Political campaigns called for a "rights not charity" approach' (Mercer, 2002: 117). The logic of this approach suggests the need for a concept analogous to 'sexism' or 'racism' to describe the ideological system which justifies the exclusion of disabled people from society: hence 'disablism'.

In fact 'disablism' has been responsible for rather more active forms of oppression than just the failure to provide access. To give an example: the fact that Winston Churchill in 1909 suggested the sterilisation of 'mental defectives' is sometimes mentioned (see Churchill Papers, CHAR 12/1/3, at www-archives.chu.cam.ac.uk). What is not so often mentioned is that he thought (possibly correctly) that his proposal was more humane than another alternative, which was to effectively incarcerate large numbers of men and women (including many we would now regard as having extremely mild learning difficulties, or as simply not being of very high intelligence), in institutions where the sexes were rigidly segregated to prevent them from reproducing. *This second alternative was actually implemented and many people institutionalised in this way remained so into the 1980s.*

In the face of a history of humiliating and infantilising treatment of disabled people, and their continued exclusion from full participation in society, the social worker seeking to counter 'disablism' has to try to radically rethink their traditional role from paternalistic helper to enabler, or advocate, or ally (see, for instance Brandon et al., 1995).

Age

Age is a common basis for gratuitous and unwarranted discrimination and has accordingly been given its own 'ism'.

Ageism

The term ageism was first coined by Robert Butler in the 1960s. He defined it as a process of stereotyping and discrimination against people because they are old ... (*Blackwell Encyclopaedia of Social Work*, ed. Davies 2000: 7)

Butler used the term to describe the negative effect this form of stereotyping had on a section of the society, typically the ageing population who were seen as redundant and to some a burden on society.

Although the term was coined to refer to discrimination against old people, discrimination against people on grounds of age is not necessarily confined to the elderly. One could argue that children in particular are discriminated against on grounds of age.

The kind of infantilising and humiliating treatment that has been meted out in the past to people with disabilities has also been suffered by old people. At times some residential homes for the elderly can seem more like warehouses for the storage of entities who would otherwise be an inconvenience and a worry for relatives and neighbours than genuine homes for people. When this happens it surely constitutes a breakdown of 'respect for persons', with people no longer really being valued as 'ends' in their own right, except in so far as society recognises an obligation to keep them physically alive. The shift from autonomous human being to an entity whose fate is to be decided by others to suit their own convenience is a shift which many old people must experience, to a greater or lesser extent, and in various ways. And this kind of discrimination, it can be argued, occurs at a structural as well as at an individual level, as is illustrated by political discourse about the problems of an ageing population and the burden it places on the rest of society.

The ethical challenge for social workers working with older people is to carry out their function of managing and distributing limited care resources while still holding on to the idea that old people are people, entitled to their own views and opinions, and not just logistical problems to be solved.

When it comes to the other end of the age range – children – age discrimination takes a number of forms. Children, specially small children, live pretty much under the control of adults, and their voices can very easily go unheard, as is illustrated by the fact that the extent of physical abuse and sexual abuse of children in society has only really been understood in the last half-century. Like social workers who work with old people, social workers working with children have to try hard not to be deflected from attending to the needs and perspectives of children by the needs and views of other, often more vocal, family members or indeed by the demands of other professionals and their own agencies. They also have to be careful to remember, as Dame Elizabeth Butler-Sloss commented in the Cleveland report, that 'The child is a person and not an object of concern' (1987: 245).

The benefits of difference and diversity

We have been discussing the ways that people from various groups may be discriminated against and oppressed by other groups. But it would be a rather negative and one-sided view of difference and diversity that dwelt only on the problems it causes for those who are seen as 'different'. As we said at the beginning of the chapter, difference is a challenge for all of us, but we should not lose sight of the fact that difference is also a source of comfort and delight. Within every family and every group of friends, people are different from one another in all kinds of ways and this is something that gives us pleasure and is often helpful to us, even if it is sometimes the source too of tensions and misunderstanding.

Presented with a salad, most of us would feel disappointed if it contained nothing but identical lettuce leaves. In the same way, most of us would find life rather sad and dull if we never met people who differed from us in any way. So working with difference and diversity is not just a matter of challenging unfair discrimination, important though that is. It is also a matter of positively celebrating diversity.

Genuine respect for persons entails accepting difference, both at an individual level and at the level of structures, policies and institutions, and it means recognising that people in different circumstances and with different backgrounds have different needs. It also means recognising that people in different circumstances also have different things to *contribute*, and that society as a whole benefits from diversity. It is a cliché but nevertheless entirely true that 'it takes all sorts to make a world'.

Chapter summary

The areas covered in this chapter have been:

- Differences, diversity and discrimination
- Being discriminating and being discriminatory
- Dimensions of difference

> ➢ Ethnicity/race
> ➢ Class
> ➢ Gender
> ➢ Disability
> ➢ Age

- The benefits of difference and diversity

This chapter has looked at the implications for social work practice raised by the existence of difference and diversity in society. We have discussed ethnicity, class, gender, disability, age and (in Chapter 3) religion as bases for discrimination. We could also have discussed sexual orientation and the discrimination faced by gay and lesbian people as a result of homophobia. We could have discussed sectarianism. Or we could have discussed discrimination faced by people with mental health problems. The potential list is endless, because any way in which human beings differ from one another is potentially a source of discrimination or a basis for oppression.

Social work is a profession which in large part deals with people who in one way or other are marked out as different and are to various degrees excluded from the mainstream of society. The challenge for ethical social work practice is to operate in a way which as far as possible challenges and reduces that exclusion, rather than in a way that confirms and legitimises it.

We concluded this chapter, though, by pointing out that it would be rather negative to confine our thinking about difference and diversity simply to problems of discrimination and oppression. It is important too to recognise that difference and diversity are necessary and valuable, even 'the spice of life'.

Afterword

An increasing emphasis in contemporary social work on prescribed assessment frameworks and on 'evidence-based' practice might, to a superficial observer, suggest that social work is becoming more 'objective', more 'technical' and less concerned with questions to do with values and ethics. This would be entirely mistaken, however, for such questions remain as central to social work practice now as they have ever been. In fact it is quite simply impossible to imagine a form of social work that is value-free. A social worker who *believed* that her actions were value-free would in reality simply be a social worker who had not learned to reflect on the values which she in fact applied every day in her work. Our aim in this book has been primarily to encourage such reflection, rather than to dictate what a social worker's value base should be.

One of the challenges for the two authors of this book has been the realisation that, while we both agree on the importance of values and ethics in social work, our own value systems are not identical and are based on very different underlying assumptions. We find it reassuring that, nevertheless, we have been able to work together very amicably and to come up with a text whose contents we can both feel comfortable with. It occurs to us that this sort of experience is not confined to the joint writing of books. In social work, in multidisciplinary work and indeed in life generally, values and ethics are central to who we are, indispensable parts of what it means to be human, and yet at the same time we must work with the fact that other people's values are seldom precisely the same as our own.

We hope that some of the material in this book will have prompted discussions which will allow readers both to explore their differences with others and to find ways of working together constructively in spite of those differences.

References

Amphlett, S. (2000) 'System abuse: social violence and families,' in Payne, H. and Littlechild, B. (2000) *Ethical Practice and the Abuse of Power in Social Responsibility.* London: Jessica Kingsley, pp. 175–209.

Banks, S. (2001) *Ethics and Values in Social Work*, 2nd Edition. Basingstoke: Palgrave.

Beckett, C. (2002) 'The witch hunt metaphor (and accusations against residential care workers)', *British Journal of Social Work*, 32 (5), 621–8.

Beckett, C. and McKeigue, B. (2003) 'Children in limbo: cases where court decisions have taken two years or more', *Adoption and Fostering*, 27 (3), 31–40.

Biestek, F. (1963) *The Casework Relationship*. St Leonard's: Allen and Unwin.

Brandon, D. (1990) *Zen in the Art of Helping*. Harmondsworth: Arkana.

Brandon, D. (2000) *Tao of Survival: Spirituality in Social Care and Helping*. Birmingham: Venture.

Brandon, D., Brandon, A. and Brandon, T. (1995) *Advocacy: Power to People with Disabilities*. Birmingham: Venture.

British Association of Social Workers (2002) *Code of Ethics for Social Work.* Birmingham: BASW.

Bullock, A. and Stallybrass, O. (1977) *Dictionary of Modern Thought*. London: Fontana.

Butler-Sloss, Lord Justice E. (1987) *Report of the Inquiry into Child Abuse in Cleveland.* London: HMSO.

Butrym, Z. (1976) *The Nature of Social Work*. Basingstoke: Macmillan.

Canda, E. (1989) 'Religious content in social work education: a comparative approach', *Journal of Social Work Education*, 30 (1), 38–45.

Care Standards Act, 2000, London: The Stationery Office.

Carers (Recognition and Services) Act, 1995, London: The Stationery Office.

CCETSW (1976) *Paper 13, Social Work Curriculum Study*. London: CCETSW.

Children Act, 1989, London: The Stationery Office.

Clark, C.L. (2000) *Social Work Ethics: Politics, Principles and Practice*. Basingstoke: Macmillan.

Clark, S. (2003) *Social Theory, Psychoanalysis and Racism*. Basingstoke: Palgrave.

Cobb, R. and Ross, M. (1997) 'Denying agenda access: strategic considerations', in Cobb, R. and Ross, M. (eds), *Cultural Strategies of Agenda Denial*. Lawrence, Kansas: University Press of Kansas, pp. 25–45.

Conrad, A. (1988) 'Ethical considerations in the psychosocial process', *Social Casework*, 69, 603–10.

Cree, V. (1995) *From Public Streets to Private Lives*. Aldershot: Avebury.

Crisp, R. (ed.) (1998) *How Should One Live? Essays on the Virtues*. Oxford: Oxford University Press.

Crisp, R. and Slote, M. (1997) *Virtue Ethics*. Oxford: Oxford University Press.

Dalrymple, J. and Burke, B. (1995) *Anti-Oppressive Practice*. Buckingham: Open University Press.

Davies, M. (ed.) (2000) *The Blackwell Encyclopaedia of Social Work*. Oxford: Blackwell.

Dawood, N. (trans.) (1990) *The Koran*, 5th Edition. London: Penguin.

Day, P. (1989) *A New History of Social Welfare*. Englewood Cliffs, NJ: Prentice-Hall.

de Shazer, S. (1985) *Keys to Solution in Brief Therapy*. New York: Norton.

Department for Education and Skills (DfES) (2003) *Every Child Matters*. London: The Stationery Office.

Department of Health (1991) *The Children Act 1989 Guidance and Regulations: Volume (3) Family Placements*. London: HMSO.

Department of Health (1999) *Effective Care Co-ordination in Mental Health Services: Modernising the Care Programme Approach*. London: The Stationery Office.

Department of Health (2000) *Framework for the Assessment of Children in Need and their Families*. London: The Stationery Office.

Dominelli, L. (1997) *Anti-Racist Social Work*, 2nd Edition. Basingstoke: Macmillan.

Downrie, R.S. and Telfer, E. (1980) *Caring and Curing: a Philosophy of Medicine and Social Work*. London: Methuen.

Dubois, B. and Miley, K. (1996) *Social Work: an Empowering Profession*. Harlow: Allyn and Bacon.

Fanon, F. (1967) *Black Skin, White Masks*. New York: Grove Press.

Foucault, M. (1980) 'Truth and Power', in Michel Foucault, *Power/Knowledge*, ed. Colin Gordon. Hemel Hempstead: Harvester Wheatsheaf.

Foucault, M. (1999) *The Foucault Reader*, ed. P. Rabinow. Harmondsworth: Penguin.

Frankl, V. (1968) *The Doctor and the Soul*. New York: Knopf.

Freire, P. (1993) *Pedagogy of the Oppressed*. Harmondsworth: Penguin.

General Social Care Council (GSCC) (2002) *Draft Codes of Conduct and Practice for Social Care Workers and Employers of Social Care Workers*. London: GSCC.

General Social Care Council (GSCC) (2003) *Codes of Practice for Social Care Workers and Employers*. London: General Social Care Council.

Gibbons, J., Gallagher, B., Bell, C. and Gordon, D. (1995) *Development after Physical Abuse in Early Childhood*. London: HMSO.

Girling, J. (1993) 'Who gets what – and why? Ethical frameworks for managers', in Allen, I. (ed.), *Rationing of Health and Social Care*. London: Policy Services Institute, pp. 40–7.

Guterman, N. (2001) *Stopping Child Maltreatment before it Starts: Emerging Horizons in Early Home Visitation Services*. Thousand Oaks, CA: Sage.

Holland, T. (1989) 'Values, faith and professional practice', *Social Thought*, 15 (1), 29–41.

Holmes, A. (1984) *Ethics: Approaching Moral Decisions*. Nottingham: Inter-Varsity Press.

Horne, M. (1999) *Values in Social Work*, 2nd Edition. Aldershot: Ashgate Arena.

Houston, S. (2001) 'Beyond social constructionism: critical realism and social work', *British Journal of Social Work*, 31, 845–61.

Hudson, M. (1995) *Managing without Profit: The Art of Managing Third Sector Organizations*. Harmondsworth: Penguin.

Hursthouse, R. (1998) 'Normative virtue ethics', in Crisp, R. (ed.), *How Should One Live? Essays on the Virtues*. Oxford: Oxford University Press, pp. 19–36.

Jordan, B. (1991) 'Competencies and values', *Social Work Education*, 10 (1), 5–11.

Kalish, R.A. and Reynolds, D.K. (1976) *Death and Ethnicity: a Psychocultural Study*. Los Angeles: University of Southern California Press.

Kant, I. (1979 [1779]) *Lectures on Ethics*, trans. L. Infield. London: Methuen.

Keating, F. (1997) *Developing an Integrated Approach to Oppression*. London: CCETSW.

Laming, Lord H. (2003) *Report of an Inquiry into the Death of Victoria Climbié*. London: The Stationery Office.

Leighton, N., Stalley, R. and Watson, J. (1982) *Rights and Responsibilities*. London: Heinemann.

Lewis, J. and Glennerster, H. (1996) *Implementing the New Community Care*. Buckingham: Open University Press.

Loewenberg, F. (1988) *Religion and Social Work Practice in Contemporary Society*. New York: Columbia University Press.

McBeath, G. and Webb, S. (2002) 'Virtue, ethics and social work: being lucky, realistic and not doing one's duty', *British Journal of Social Work*, 32, 1015–36.

McCaffrey, T. (1998) 'The pain of managing', in Foster, A. and Zagier Roberts, V. (eds), *Managing Mental Health in the Community*. London: Routledge.

Macpherson, W. (1999) *The Stephen Lawrence Inquiry: Report of an Inquest*. London: The Stationery Office.

Mandela, N. (1994) *Long Walk to Freedom*. London: Abacus.

Marx, K. and Engels, F. (1967 [1848]) *The Communist Manifesto*, introduced by A.J.P. Taylor. Harmondsworth: Pelican.

Mental Health Act, 1983, London: The Stationery Office.

Mercer, G. (2002) 'Disability and oppression: changing theories and practices', in Tomlinson, D. and Trew, W. (eds), *Equalising Opportunities, Minimising Oppression. A Critical Review of Anti-discriminatory Policies in Health and Social Welfare*. London: Routledge, pp. 117–33.

NHS and Community Care Act, 1990, London: The Stationery Office.

Norman, R. (1998) *The Moral Philosophers: An Introduction to Ethics*, 2nd Edition. Oxford: Oxford University Press.

Office for National Statistics (1999) *Census News* (41), March 14th, London: The Stationery Office.

Olsen, J., Richardson, J., Dolan, P. and Menzel, P. (2003) 'The moral relevance of personal characteristics in setting healthcare priorities', *Social Science and Medicine*, 57, 1163–72.

Ovretveit, J. (1998) *Evaluating Health Interventions*. Buckingham: Open University Press.

Parton, N. and O'Byrne, P. (2000) *Constructive Social Work: Towards a New Practice*. Basingstoke: Macmillan.

Payne, M. (1997) *Modern Social Work Theory*, 2nd Edition, Basingstoke: Macmillan.

Philpot, T. (1986) *Social Work: A Christian Perspective*. Hertford: Lion Publishing.

PIU (Performance and Innovation Unit) (2000) *Prime Minister's Review on Adoption*. London: Cabinet Office.

Proudhon, P-J. (1994) *What is Property?* ed. D. Kelley and B. Smith. Cambridge: Cambridge University Press.

Raban, J. (2003) 'The Greatest Gulf', *The Guardian*, 19 April 2003.

Rachels, J. (1999) *The Elements of Moral Philosophy*, 3rd Edition. Boston: McGraw Hill.

Reid, W. (1978) *The Task-Centered System*. New York: Columbia University Press.

Roakeach, M. (1973) *The Nature of Human Values*. New York: Free Press.

Rogers, C. (1967) *On Becoming a Person: A Therapist's View of Psychotherapy*. London: Constable & Robinson.

Schön, D. (1991) *The Reflective Practitioner: How Professionals Think in Action*. Aldershot: Arena.

Shor, R. (2000) 'Child maltreatment: differences in perceptions between parents in low income and middle income neighbourhoods', *British Journal of Social Work*, 30, 165–78.

Silavwe, G. (1995) 'The need for a new social work persepective in an African setting: the case of social casework in Zambia', *British Journal of Social Work*, 25, 71–84.

Sollod, R. (1992) 'The hollow curriculum: the place of religion and spirituality in society is too often missing', *Chronicle of Higher Education*, 38 (28), A60.

Solomon, B. (1976) *Black Empowerment: Social Work in Oppressed Communities*. New York: Columbia University Press.

Thoburn, J. (2002) 'Out-of-home care for the abused or neglected child: research, policy and practice', in Wilson, K. and James, A. (eds), *The Child Protection Handbook*, 2nd Edition. Edinburgh: Baillière Tindall, pp. 514–37.

Thompson, N. (1992) *Existentialism and Social Work*. Aldershot: Avebury.

Thompson, N. (2001) *Anti-discriminatory Practice*, 3rd Edition. Basingstoke: Palgrave.

Thompson, N. (2002) 'Developing anti-discriminatory practice', in Tomlinson, D. and Trew, W. (eds), *Equalising Opportunities, Minimising Oppression: a Critical Review of Anti-Discriminatory Policies in Health and Social Welfare*. London: Routledge, pp. 41–55.

Timms, N. (1983) *Social Work Values: an Enquiry*. London: Routledge.

Trevithick, P. (2000) *Social Work Skills: a Practice Handbook*. Buckingham: Open University Press.

Walker, R. (1998) *Kant*. London: Phoenix.

Walker, S. and Beckett, C. (2003) *Social Work Assessment and Intervention*. Lyme Regis: Russell House Publishing.

Wilding, P. (1982) *Professional Power and Social Welfare*. London: Routledge and Kegan Paul.

Web references

Bar Council: www.barcouncil.org.uk

Barnado's: www.barnados.org.uk

British Association of Social Workers: www.basw.co.uk

British Medical Association: www.bma.org.uk

Churchill Papers, CHAR 12/1/3, at www-archives.chu.cam.ac.uk

General Medical Council: www.gmc-uk.org

General Social Care Council: www.gscc.org.uk

International Federation of Social Workers: www.ifsw.org

Law Society: www.lawsoc.org.uk

National Association of Social Workers (USA): www.socialworkers.org

National Society for the Prevention of Cruelty to Children: www.nspcc.org.uk

Royal Institution of Chartered Surveyors: www.rics.org.uk

Index

Compiled by INDEXING SPECIALISTS
(UK) Ltd, Regent House, Hove Street, Hove,
East Sussex BN3 2DW. Tel: 01273 738299.
email: richardr@indexing.co.uk Website:
www.indexing.co.uk

FEMINIST ISSUES
in
LITERARY
SCHOLARSHIP